The best of SOUTH AFRICA

PETER JOYCE

NEW HOLLAND

GLOBETROTTER™

First edition published in 2004
by New Holland Publishers (UK) Ltd
London • Cape Town • Sydney • Auckland
10 9 8 7 6 5 4 3 2 1

website: www.newhollandpublishers.com

Garfield House, 86 Edgware Road
London W2 2EA
United Kingdom

80 McKenzie Street
Cape Town 8001
South Africa

14 Aquatic Drive
Frenchs Forest, NSW 2086
Australia

218 Lake Road
Northcote, Auckland
New Zealand

Distributed in the USA by
The Globe Pequot Press, Connecticut

ISBN 1 84330 617 4

Front Cover: *Pilgrim's Rest, Mpumalanga.*
Title Page: *People of South Africa.*

Publishing Manager (UK): Simon Pooley
Publishing Manager (SA): Thea Grobbelaar
DTP Cartographic Manager: Genené Hart
Editors: Sean Fraser, Melany McCallum
Designer: Lellyn Creamer
Cover design: Lellyn Creamer, Nicole Engeler
Cartographer: Nicole Engeler
Picture Researcher: Shavonne Johannes

Reproduction by Fairstep (Cape Town) and
Hirt & Carter (Pty) Ltd, Cape Town
Printed and bound in Hong Kong by Sing Cheong
Printing Co. Ltd.

CONTENTS

MAKE THE MOST OF YOUR GUIDE

Reading these two pages will help you to get the most out of your guide and save you time when using it. Sites discussed in the text are cross-referenced with the cover maps – for example, the reference 'Map A–C3' refers to the Johannesburg City Centre Map (Map A), column C, row 3. Use the Map Plan below to quickly locate the map you need.

MAP PLAN

Outside Back Cover   Outside Front Cover

Inside Front Cover   Inside Back Cover

THE BIGGER PICTURE

Key to Map Plan
A – Johannesburg City Centre
B – Pretoria (Tshwane)
C – Sun City
D – Around Johannesburg
E – South Africa
F – Western Cape
G – Cape Peninsula
H – Cape Town City Centre
I – V & A Waterfront
J – Garden Route
K – KwaZulu-Natal
L – Port Elizabeth
M– Durban City Centre

Key to Symbols

⊠ — address

☎ — telephone

℘ — fax

🖳 — website

⌂ — e-mail address

⊕ — opening times

🚌 — tour

💰 — entry fee

🍽 — restaurants nearby

Map Legend

motorway	main road — **Adderley**
national road	other road — Corporation
principal road	mall — ST GEORGE'S MALL
main road	built-up area
minor road	one-way arrow
mountain pass	shopping centre — Ⓢ
railway	hotel — Ⓗ PARK INN
river	viewpoint
route number — N1	battle site
city — CAPE TOWN	place of interest — God's Window
major town — ⊙ Paarl	parking area — Ⓟ
town — Ⓞ Hout Bay	building of interest — Melrose House
large village — ◎ Tzaneen	library
village — ○ Onrus	post office — ⊠
airport — ✈ ✈	tourist information — ⓘ
toll road — Ⓣ	place of worship — △
mountain peak — Giant's Castle ▲ 3312 m	police station — ●
rest camp — ⌂	bus terminus — 🚌
cave — 🔴	hospital — ⊕
park & garden — Company's Gardens	

Keep us Current

Travel information is apt to change, which is why we regularly update our guides. We'd be most grateful to receive feedback from you if you've noted something we should include in our updates. If you have any new information, please share it with us by writing to the Publishing Manager, Globetrotter, at the office nearest to you (addresses on the imprint page of this guide). The most significant contribution to each new edition will be rewarded with a free copy of the updated guide.

Above: *The Garden
Route is one of
South Africa's most
popular tourist
destinations.*

Facts and Figures
• **Highest mountains**
are the Drakensberg,
peaking at Champagne
Castle (at 3376m;
11,077ft), which is just
one of the buttresses.
• **Longest river** is the
Gariep (Orange), which
flows for 2250km (1400
miles) east to west.
• **Largest waterfall**
(and one of the world's
six largest) is Augrabies
on the Gariep; a series
of 19 cataracts tumble
146m (479ft).
• **Deepest gorge** is
the Blyde River Canyon
in Mpumalanga – up to
800m (2625ft) deep
and 1.5km (1 mile)
wide in places.

OVERVIEW

South Africa covers an area of well over a
million square kilometres (386,000 square
miles) of the southern subcontinent. A
country rich in diversity, it boasts not only a
bewildering mix of culture and language,
but also a varied character – in the cities
and the nature of the land. Eastwards from
the metropolis of **Johannesburg** lies the
rugged **Escarpment**, which falls rapidly
away to the subtropical **Lowveld** with its
world-famous **Kruger National Park**. To the
south lies **KwaZulu-Natal**, with its own
bushveld, wetland and marine reserves.
Durban, a harbour city fringed by golden
beaches, is the third largest conurbation in
the country. Further south is the **Eastern
Cape's** spectacular **Wild Coast**, and along
the southern shores the **Garden Route**, a
place of gentle beauty, comprising seaside
towns, forests and lakes, against a backdrop
of the **Outeniqua** range. A journey through
the rich **Western Cape** farmlands and along
the southern seaboard culminates in the
Cape Peninsula and the city of **Cape Town**,
at the foot of **Table Mountain**, and its surrounds – the **Winelands** – a series of craggy
peaks and secluded valleys with vineyards,
orchards and historic homesteads.

The Land

In broad terms, South Africa can be divided
into two regions. The greater is the semi-
circular interior plateau, varying in altitude
from the central region of the **Great Karoo**
(a vast, flat semidesert) to the **Drakensberg**
in the east (the loftiest of the mountains of
the **Great Escarpment**). The second region is
a **coastal belt** fringing the plateau.

Climate

Weather patterns vary dramatically, but there are three broad rainfall regions. The **southwestern** tip has a winter rainfall (May to August), while the **southern and eastern coastal belts** enjoy perennial showers, which are heavy – almost tropical – in KwaZulu-Natal, especially in summer. Rains on the central plateau and Lowveld come irregularly, with summer thunderstorms.

The mean annual rainfall is just 464mm (18in), and only a third of the land gets enough rain for non-irrigated farming; the perennial rivers are subject to seasonal flow.

Plant Life

Vegetation ranges from **succulents**, **aloes** and spring-flowering **desert annuals** on the parched western seaboard and the vast west-central wastelands to mountain pines and dense lowland **bushveld** in the moist northeast. Much of the plateau consists of **grasslands**, and there are few natural forests. Along Indian Ocean shoreline there are patches of evergreen **subtropical trees** and, in the swampier areas, **mangroves**.

Animal Kingdom

South Africa's magnificent wildlife heritage is at its most spectacular in the big-game areas of **Mpumalanga** and **KwaZulu-Natal** – areas popular among international visitors. In terms of species diversity, South Africa ranks third in the world, and is perhaps best known for the huge and impressive **Kruger National Park** – home of the Big Five (lion, leopard, rhino, elephant and buffalo).

Spot the Big Five

Top of the game-viewing list are the Big Five, all of which can be spotted in the Kruger National Park.
• The **lion**, largest of the carnivores, is most active at night.
• The shy and solitary **leopard** is a nocturnal hunter. Its dappled coat provides camouflage.
• Some 7500 or more **elephant** roam in the Kruger National Park.
• The **white rhino** is grey identified by its square-lipped mouth. The smaller **black rhino** is recognized by its 'hooked' upper lip.
• The placid **buffalo** can be very dangerous when threatened.

Below: *A male elephant weighing 6000kg (13,200lb) can consume 300kg (660lb) of grass, shoots and bark every day.*

Warrior Supreme
When Shaka became chief in 1816, the Zulu numbered just 1500 people – but within a few years he controlled the entire eastern (KwaZulu-Natal) seaboard. The keys to this expansion were the weapons and techniques he introduced to his army.
• The assegai, a short, stabbing weapon that replaced the spears, which had been hurled from long distances.
• He split young men of the clans into regiments according to age, ensuring loyalty to the throne rather than to the headman.
• The battle formation (known as the impi), comprising a 'chest' for frontal attack and two encirclement 'horns'.

Below: *This monument to the Anglo-Boer War is situated in Graaf Reniet.*

History in Brief

Millennia ago, bands of nomadic **San** hunter-gatherers roamed the great spaces in search of sustenance. About 2000 years ago some concentrated in loose federations but eventually divided, some migrating to the Cape Peninsula. Meanwhile, **Bantu-speakers** – who used iron and kept cattle – occupied parts of what is now Zimbabwe, to be followed, around AD1100, by a stronger migratory wave through the interior and down the east coast. By the 1600s, the **Xhosa** were advancing south on a collision course with **European colonists**.

The Clash of Cultures

In April 1652, **Jan van Riebeeck** docked in Table Bay to set up a victualling station for the Dutch East India Company's fleets en route to the East. Eventually, officials began to farm and **slaves** from other parts of Africa and the Far East were imported to work the land. The Cape expanded steadily as '**trekboers**' began to push the borders ever outward. In the east they came up against the Xhosa, and competed for grazing. In 1779 the first 'frontier war' erupted.

Colonial Expansion

In the late 1700s, the Netherlands began to decline and the **British** took control of the Cape in 1795. They later withdrew for about eight years, but returned in 1806 to rule for the rest of the 19th century, during which white settlement expanded to cover the entire southern region.

The Great Trek

In the 1830s, many of the Cape's Dutch settlers headed for the interior in the **Great Trek**, eventually taking control of much of the territory north of the Orange River and establishing the Boer republics of the **Orange Free State** and the **Transvaal**.

War and Union

But the discovery of diamonds in Kimberley in the 1860s, and gold on the Witwatersrand 25 years later, destroyed any chance of peace between Boer and Briton and the two countries went to war again.

The **Anglo-Boer War** of 1899–1902 left a legacy of bitterness, but finally, on 31 May 1910, the former Boer republics (Transvaal and Orange Free State) and the British colonies (Cape and Natal) became the **Union of South Africa**. Black people had, however, not been consulted and had no democratic rights within the new order.

The Road to Democracy

In 1948, the **National Party** established its apartheid policy – restrictive, racially based laws that segregated black and white, and deprived the people of South Africa of basic rights. In the struggle for freedom that was to shape the country for nearly 50 years, activists in the **African National Congress** – notably **Nelson Mandela**, released from prison after 27 years – emerged to help lead South Africa to **democracy** in 1994.

Above: *Nelson Mandela, one-time 'political' prisoner on Robben Island, became the nation's first democratically elected president.*

Steps to Freedom
Among the highlights of the liberation struggle in the apartheid years were the award of the **Nobel Peace Prize** to **Chief Albert Luthuli**, who became president of the African National Congress (ANC) in 1952, and the signing of the **Freedom Charter** in 1955. The Charter, a crucial document that provided the framework of future protest, stated that South Africa belonged to all its people, and went on to advocate a nonracial democracy, equal rights, educational and job opportunities.

Government and Economy

The new govern-ment; the economy; the restructuring of society – these issues are fundamental to South Africa even 10 years into democracy – a mix of First World sophistication and Third World under-development.

Above: *Gold Reef City mine recreates early Johannesburg, complete with gold pouring.*

Foreign Earnings
- Precious metals (39%)
- Base metals and articles thereof (14%)
- Minerals (11%)
- Vehicles and machinery (6%)
- Chemicals (5%)
- Agricultural products, such as (animals, pro-duce, fats and oils (5%)
- Paper products (3%)
- Textiles, clothing and footwear (3%)
- Prepared foodstuffs (and tobacco) (3%)
- Wood, leather and their products (1%)
- Rubber, plastic and their products (1%)
- Other (including, among others, scientific equipment) (9%)

Wealth and Poverty

On one hand, South Africa has immense natural resources, employs the latest tech-nologies, and supports advanced industrial and commercial structures. On the other, the standard of education among black South Africans is low; there are too few jobs and services and the 'poverty cycle' is very real, threatening the nation's stability. What nearly everyone is agreed on is that the country's wealth has to be divided more equitably. Organized labour pushes for central planning within a socialist-type command economy; government and busi-ness favour the creation of wealth (and jobs) through the free play of market forces.

Contributions to South Africa's economic wellbeing take no account of the dynamic 'informal economy' – home-based business, market trading, hawking, minibus services, crafts and *shebeens* (bars) – tiny ventures that are thought to account for around 30 per cent of total domestic income. These provide work, generate wealth, develop skills and help pioneer the economic future.

The People

More than a third of South Africa's population of 44.8 million lives in and around the cities and towns, largest of which are **Johannesburg**, **Pretoria** and their urban neighbours. Sprawling untidily around every town and city are what used to be called 'African' townships, many of which started life as 'locations' for cheap and temporary labour – makeshift, soulless places in the early days, virtually devoid of any real civic amenities. **Soweto**, close to Johannesburg, is the best known. However, urban conditions are improving – more permanent areas, though overcrowded, have basic services, electricity, schools, clinics, community centres, sports fields, clubs and shebeens. In some places the streets are paved, and there are pockets of substantial residences – notably in Soweto – for the rapidly emerging African middle class.

But development can't keep pace with the numbers of people driven from a countryside that can no longer support them, and who are lured to the towns by the prospect of jobs and a better life. Vast '**squatter camps**' have proliferated around established townships, packed settlements of rudimentary homes, and rows of shelters thrown together. Some 700,000 rural folk are migrating to the cities each year, around half the country's population now resides in and around the urban areas, and 'urban drift' – alongside **unemployment**, the shortage of skills and the **HIV/AIDS** pandemic – ranks among the country's most pressing problems.

Work for the People

According to the 2001 census, published in 2003, unemployment rates in the provinces were as follows:
- Limpopo (48.8%)
- KwaZulu-Natal (48.7%)
- Eastern Cape (54.6%)
- North West (43.8%)
- Mpumalanga (41.1%)
- Free State (43%)
- Gauteng (36.4%)
- Northern Cape (33.4%)
- Western Cape (26.1%)

The 2001 census revealed that the rate of joblessness among population groups were as follows:
- black (50.2%)
- coloured (27%)
- Indian (16.9%)
- white (6.3%)

Below: *Standard housing in Soweto, although an ever-growing number of homes are now quite comfortable.*

Traditional Healers

Diviners (mediums) play a significant role in traditional culture. Known to Zulus as **sangomas**, they are recruited by the ancestors, undergo a rigorous apprenticeship, and act as intermediaries between the living and their forefathers. Techniques vary but, generally, practitioners predict, divine and heal a multitude of ills of the psychological or social kind.

The herbalist, on the other hand, fills the role of doctor in traditional society, and his/her function is to cure physical ailments, prescribing from a wide range of herbs, tree bark and other medicinal flora of the veld, many of which are known to have valuable curative properties.

Below: *The picturesque Belvedere Church at Knysna.*

Language

South Africa's cultural mix is reflected in its variety of languages and dialects. **English** and **Afrikaans** were once the only official languages, but all **11 spoken languages** are now official, and themost prominent media outlet – the South African Broadcasting Corporation (**SABC**), operates three television channels (SABC1, -2, -3) and numerous regional radio services. There are a number of independent radio stations, and privately run television channels include **M-Net** (subscription) and **e-tv** (free-to-air).

Religion

Religion is determined largely by cultural origin. Biggest of the Christian groups are the **Dutch Reformed** churches, which have Calvinist roots, followed by the **Roman Catholic**, **Methodist**, **Anglican**, **Presbyterian** and **Baptist** congregations. Around 100,000 South Africans are **Jewish**. **Hindus** number nearly 600,000 and **Moslems** 400,000, both concentrated in KwaZulu-Natal, although many in the Cape also follow Islam.

Combining Christianity with elements of **traditional belief** are over 2000 indigenous, independent churches, most of them in Limpopo and Mpumalanga. The **Zion Christian Church** (ZCC) is the biggest. Most of the groups believe in prophet-healers and some wear colourful robes.

Many of the African traditional beliefs remain influential, even among mainstream Christians.

Traditional Cultures

Although most of South Africa's larger settlements are indistinguishable from any American or European cities, there are indeed pockets of exotic culture and old Africa still survives in many country areas.

The **Asian** community retains much of the customs of the Indian mainland, and society is strongly unified, organized according to the Hindu or Moslem faith, each of which has strict rules.

The '**Cape Malays**' are largely descended from slaves brought from Ceylon and the Indonesian islands. This devout, integrated society of around 200,000 has evolved a distinctive tradition and cuisine.

Some **Ndebele** village women still wear anklets and necklaces that can never be removed, and paint their homesteads in geometric patterns. The **Swazi** celebrate unity and the rebirth of their chiefs in a zestful marathon of song and dance. **Venda** girls perform the domba snake-dance to mark their entry into womanhood. **Xhosa** women are famed for their beadwork (patterns represent status as well as identity), and young country boys still go through a long and painful initiation ritual.

In KwaZulu-Natal you may see beehive huts made by **Zulu** craftsmen – as well as beaded headdresses and the regalia of a fast disappearing age. Remnants of ancient Africa are everywhere, although much of what remains is laid on for tourists.

Above: *A drummer daubed with traditional war paint.*

Township Jive

With the movement to the cities, a new sound has emerged. Called **Mbaqanga**, it draws much from the original music of Africa, but has been influenced by American big-band jazz and soul, giving it a vibrant character. Township music defies any simple definition – there are too many ingredients, too many roots – but unmistakable is the throbbing undertone of Africa.

'Mbaqanga' is an African word for maize bread and, like the food it describes, it feeds a deep hunger.

Above: *The J.G. Strijdom tower is the tallest in the city.*

Tourism Johannesburg
✉ Village Walk, Sandton
☎ (011) 784-1352

Johannesburg International Airport
☎ (011) 921-6262

Gauteng Tourism
✉ Rosebank Mall, Rosebank
☎ (011) 327-2000

Satour
(national tourism body)
☎ (011) 778-8000

Info Africa
🖥 www.infoafrica.co.za

Market Theatre
See page 71

Gold Reef City
See page 46

☆ *See* Map A/D   ★ ★ ★

JOHANNESBURG

Although Johannesburg, capital of Gauteng and South Africa's largest metropolis, has little claim to beauty, it is in many ways a microcosm of the country; a kaleidoscope of past and future: modern towers juxtaposed with survivors of the city's gold-rush days, and pockets of African muti shops.

Central Johannesburg, with tall buildings, congested thoroughfares and pavements, is known as Africa's Manhattan, and there's something left for every visitor, especially in the inner-city **Hillbrow** and **Yeoville**, and in the ambitious **Newtown** redevelopment area, where you'll find the Cultural Precinct and exuberant nightlife and 'arts hotspots'.

The **Market Theatre Complex** on Mary Fitzgerald Square is a lively complex of four auditoriums, markets, boutiques, bookshop, bistros and live experimental theatre.

Gold Reef City (see page 46), a reconstruction of early Johannesburg, is located on the old Crown Mines site. Visitors can descend a mineshaft to explore the underground workings, watch gold being poured, or even try their luck at the casino. Other attractions are traditional dances; tram and horse-drawn omnibus rides; a Victorian funfair, pub and tea parlour; replicas of an early theatre, stock exchange, newspaper office; house museums furnished in period style; and many attractive specialty shops (diamonds, leatherware, pottery, glassware, lace, coins, stamps, curios). The Crown Restaurant serves gourmet fare; the period-style Gold Reef City Hotel offers standard to luxurious accommodation.

⭐ *See* Map B3   ★★★

SOWETO

South Africa's best-known 'black' city straddles nearly 100km² (39 sq miles) of dusty terrain southwest of Johannesburg. Much of it is electrified, some streets are paved, and more prosperous residents have large and attractive homes. Formal development has been slow, and the majority of Sowetans live in matchbox houses in overcrowded conditions that are poorly serviced. Soweto – an acronym of SOuth WEstern TOwnships – was designed as a dormitory town. Most workers still commute daily by train and minibus to the city and other nearby centres. Big business has passed Soweto by (until recently it was forced to do so by law), and commercial activity is represented by some 4000 'spaza' stores and the burgeoning 'informal sector' (hawking, markets, backyard industries).

Soweto has few civic amenities. The **Chris Hani-Baragwanath Hospital**, is Africa's largest, while *The Sowetan* newspaper is the country's fastest growing in circulation terms. Social life revolves around the football stadiums and grounds, the myriad *shebeens* (home bars) and up-market nightclubs and community halls. The best way to experience Soweto is with a specialist tour operator, the biggest of which is Jimmy's Face to Face Tours (excursions depart from hotels in Sandton, Rosebank and the central area). Imbizo Tours customize tours to include Soweto's lively nightlife.

Satour
(national tourism body)
☎ (011) 778-8000

Info Africa
🖥 www.infoafrica.co.za

Dumela Africa
☎ (083) 659-9928
✉ dumela@
netactive.co.za

Jimmy's Face to Face Tours
☎ (011) 331-6109

Imbizo Tours
☎ (011) 838-2667

Ma-Africa Tours
☎ (011) 984-2561

Welcome Tours & Safaris
☎ (082) 415-4325
✉ alextour@
netactive.co.za

Below: *A popular upmarket restaurant and pub in Soweto.*

See Map C   ★ ★ ★

The Palace of the Lost City
The **Palace**, an ornate affair of domes and minarets, has 350 luxurious rooms and suites, two restaurants set in exotic foliage surrounding cascading water features.

The **Valley of Waves**, an outdoor playground, incorporates waterfalls, slides, river rides, a beach and an enormous surf pool with artificially generated waves.

Sun City Hotel & Cabanas
☎ (01455) 21-000

The Palace
☎ (01455) 71-000

Cascades
☎ (01455) 73-000

Below: *The Palace of the Lost City is the centrepiece of the Lost City development at Sun City.*

SUN CITY

In the North West Province lies an opulent complex of hotels, gaming rooms, theatres, restaurants, bars, discos and shops, all set in beautifully landscaped grounds: this is the pleasure ground of Sun City, mecca for local and overseas holiday-makers. Hotels range from the family-oriented **Cabanas** through the plush Sun City complex and the **Cascades** to the magnificent Lost City – whose centrepiece is the elaborately domed and minareted **Palace of the Lost City**.

For golfers, the **Gary Player Country Club**, which hosts the annual Million Dollar Golf Challenge, has a desert-style golf course where crocodiles lie and wait.

Among Sun City's other amenities are riding stables, bowling greens and tennis and squash courts. Much revolves around attractive stretches of water – the waterscape near the Cascades, with its interlinked pools, weirs, tropical walkways and waterfowl; and **Waterworld**, a giant 'lake' for both the idle and the water-sports enthusiast.

Worth a visit is **Kwena Garden**, a 'prehistoric' reptile park and crocodile ranch.

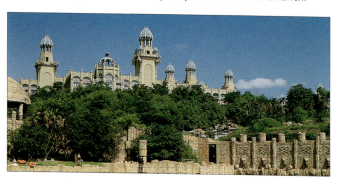

See Map E–11 ★★★

KRUGER NATIONAL PARK

This prime sanctuary, covering more than 20,000 km^2 (7720 sq miles) of the Lowveld, is pivotal to the Peace Park initiative that will connect it to others in Zimbabwe

and Mozambique so that they form the **Great Limpopo Transfrontier Park**.

Kruger can accommodate around 5000 visitors at any given time; comfort and easy access to wildlife are the keynotes. The 20 **rest camps** are tree-shaded, well-founded oases in the bushveld, linked by an extensive network of good roads. Within easy driving distance of each camp are water holes, view sites, picnic spots and a wealth of wildlife and scenic interest.

The park encompasses many different habitats and boasts Africa's greatest species diversity. Among the more than 140 mammal species are the Big Five: lion, elephant, leopard, buffalo and rhino, of both the white and black species. Other populations include some 30,000 zebra, 14,000 wildebeest and 5000 giraffe. Hippo and crocodile can be seen in and around the rivers, while thousands of antelope roam the grasslands.

The camps are pleasant, clean and safe. Daytime **game-viewing** is done from your own enclosed vehicle, along signposted routes, and there are guided night tours. Booking for accommodation is essential.

Above: *There are more than 1500 lion in the world-famous game sanctuary that is the Kruger Park.*

<u>**South African National Parks**</u>
(central reservations)
☎ (012) 428-9111
🖥 www.parks-sa.co.za
✆ reservations@parks-sa.co.za

<u>**Kruger National Park**</u>
☎ (013) 735-4030

<u>**Mpumalanga Tourism Authority**</u>
☎/📠 (013) 752-7001

✿ See Map K–A4   ★★★

THE DRAKENSBERG

South Africa's highest mountain range, the Drakensberg is a striking rampart of deep gorges, pinnacles and ridges, caves, overhangs and balancing rocks. In the winter, its upper levels lie deep in snow, but in the grasslands of the foothills below are resort hotels, many of them old, unpretentious venues for the holiday-maker. People come for the fresh, clean air; the walks, climbs and drives; trout fishing, golf, bowls and horse riding. Recommended are the Mont-aux-Sources and the Central 'Berg.

The **Royal Natal National Park** is a floral and wildlife sanctuary, home to antelope and about 200 bird species, and boasts 30 or so walks: one to the **Mont-aux-Sources** plateau and its **Amphitheatre**, another to **Tugela Falls**. Horse-riding is popular in the 'Berg, and bridle paths cross enchanting landscapes. All rides are accompanied by guides. Streams and dams offer fine fishing.

In the central 'Berg, **Giant's Castle** (part of the larger Drakensberg Park) offers scenic splendour, riding, an array of plant life and a number of raptors; bearded vultures are fed at hides or 'restaurants'. The reserve is also famed for its San rock art. Accommodation is in rustic huts, or cottages and lodges at Giant's Castle camp, or at nearby Injesuthi.

Drakensberg Tourism Association
✉ Hotel Walter, Bergville
☎ (036) 448-1557

KwaZulu-Natal Nature Conservation
(Pietermaritzburg)
☎ (033) 845-1002

Tourism KwaZulu-Natal
✉ Tourist Junction, Old Station Building, Pine Street, Durban
☎ (031) 304-7144
📠 (031) 304-8792
🖥 www.
tourism-kzn.org

Wildlife and Environment Society
☎ (031) 201-3126

South African National Parks
(central reservations)
☎ (012) 428-9111
🖥 www.parks-sa.co.za
📧 reservations@
parks-sa.co.za

Below: *The great Amphitheatre forms part of the Mont-aux-Sources massif.*

See Map J

★ ★ ★

THE GARDEN ROUTE

The Cape coastal terrace from the **Storms River** and Tsitsikamma area in the east to **Mossel Bay**, and **Heidelberg** in the western interior, is known as the Garden Route.

The **Tsitsikamma National Park** (see page 39) embraces an 80km-strip (50 miles) of coastline, its land and waters richly endowed with plant life and birds. There are also nature walks through beautiful forests and the park is traversed by the five-day 41km (25 miles) **Otter Hiking Trail**.

Plettenberg Bay is a fashionable holiday resort, and amenities include inns, holiday cottages, restaurants, shops, boutiques, bars and the famed **Beacon Island** complex. There are facilities for golf, bowls, riding, angling, diving and sailing.

Knysna is celebrated for its oysters and hardwood furniture, but its biggest drawcards are the lagoon guarded by The Heads, its waterfront and its splendid forest.

The **Wilderness Lakes Area** embraces five rivers, 28km (17 miles) of coastline and six large bodies of water: the Wilderness Lagoon, the Serpentine, Island Lake, Langvlei, Rondevlei and Swartvlei, all home to about 200 species of birds.

The Wilderness area is popular among vacationers, fishermen and bird watchers.

Above: *Plettenberg Bay is a popular mecca for holiday-makers.*

Garden Route Central Reservations
☎ (044) 874-7474 / 873-3222

Garden Route Tourism
☎ (044) 873-6314/55
📠 (044) 884-0688

Knysna Tourism
☎ (044) 382-6960

Mossel Bay Tourism Bureau
☎ (044) 691-2202

Plettenberg Bay Info
☎ (044) 533-4065

South African National Parks
(central reservations)
☎ (012) 428-9111
🖥 www.parks-sa.co.za
📧 reservations@parks-sa.co.za

Above: *The V & A Waterfont fringes the city's dockland.*

See Map G/H/I ★★★

THE CAPE PENINSULA

Cape Town's metropolis lies in the 'bowl' formed by majestic Table Mountain, its flanking peaks and Table Bay. Suburbs and satellite towns sprawl across the low-lying Cape Flats and over the **Cape Peninsula National Park**.

Among the top attractions are restaurants, hotels, craft markets and speciality shops, a lively calendar of arts, superb beaches, and the landmark **Table Mountain**, rising 1086m (3564ft) above sea level with awe-inspiring views from its flat-topped summit. Visitors may ride up in a cable car which has a revolving floor and a 360° view of the city.

Central Cape Town's attractions include **Adderley Street's** flower market, the Dutch Reformed Groote Kerk, the Slave Lodge, St George's Cathedral, St George's Mall, Greenmarket Square, Long Street, the Company's Garden and the Bo-Kaap (the 'Malay Quarter' that offers a glimpse of the exotic Cape Town of old).

High on the visitor's agenda is the **V & A Waterfront**, the multibillion-dollar redevelopment scheme on the dockland. Among its attractions are the world-class **Two Oceans Aquarium**, the larger-than-life **IMAX** cinema, the yacht basin, and **Victoria Wharf**.

Beyond the city lie the botanical gardens at **Kirstenbosch**, Constantia's **wine estates**, the golden beaches of the Atlantic seaboard and the **Cape of Good Hope Nature Reserve** with the unspoilt **Cape Point**.

Cape Town Arts
🖳 www.
gocapetown.co.za

Cape Town Tourism Visitor's Centre
✉ Burg Street,
Cape Town
☎ (021) 426-4260

MTN Flowerline
☎ (083) 910-1028

MTN Whale Hotline
☎ (073) 214-6949

Robben Island
☎ (021) 419-1300

Table Mountain Cableway
☎ (021) 424-8181
🖳 www.
tablemountain.co.za

V & A Waterfront Visitor's Centre
☎ (021) 408-7600

THE CAPE PENINSULA & THE WINELANDS

⭐ *See* Map F   ★ ★ ★

THE WINELANDS

The Cape Winelands comprise mountain ranges, valleys, vineyards, orchards and homesteads built in Cape Dutch style. Pioneer farms prospered, and as the colony expanded, small towns were founded.

The university town of **Stellenbosch** beneath the Papegaaiberg, was founded in the late 1600s. Today, many old gabled buildings – notably ,along oak-lined **Dorp Street** and in the **Village Museum** complex – reflect the origins of the town, especially its links with the wine industry, an honour shared with Paarl and Franschhoek. **Paarl** is best known for the massive pearl-like rock from which it takes its name and as the home of the **Afrikaans Language Monument**, while **Franschhoek**, 'the French quarter', is acclaimed for its outstanding restaurants and local cuisine, as well as the **Huguenot Memorial**.

All three centres are focal points of viti-culture. Each has its own established 'wine route', which showcases the finest estates of the respective wine regions. Stellenbosch boasts **Spier** and **Delhiem** among its most significant drawcards, while the Paarl route has **Nederburg**, one of the country's best-known estates.

Most of the estates and cellars offer wine tastings and tours, and most are also open on weekends. Visitors may be best advised to book.

Cape Town Tourism Visitor's Centre
✉ Burg Street, Cape Town
☎ (021) 426-4260

Felix Unite River Adventures
☎ (021) 670-1300

River Rafters
☎ (021) 712-5094

Spier Wine Estate
☎ (021) 809-1100

Stellenbosch Publicity Association
☎ (021) 883-3584 / 883-9633
📠 (021) 883-8071

Winelands Ballooning
☎ (021) 863-3192

Winelands Regional Tourism
☎ (021) 872-0686
📠 (021) 872-0534

Below: *Wooded hills and vineyards embrace the Morgenhof estate .*

See Map D–A1

★★

PILANESBERG GAME RESERVE

The Pilanesberg Game Reserve, virtually on the doorstep of **Sun City** and the **Palace of the Lost City**, stretches across a great expanse of game-rich habitat that sprawls within four concentric mountain rings, relics of an aeons-old volcano; at the centre of the bowl is **Mankwe Lake**, which is home to pods of hippopotamus.

Some 10,000 head of game are found in the park, among them both the black and white rhino, giraffe, zebra, cheetah, lion, leopard, brown hyena, elephant, warthog and a wealth of antelope. More than 300 bird species have been identified, and a visit to the aviary at **Manyane** gate should not be missed. The Pilanesberg Game Reserve is traversed by an extensive network of game-viewing roads; conducted walks and drives are available, and viewing hides have been established. Hot-air balloon trips can also be organized.

Because the reserve lies in such close proximity to metropolitan Johannesburg and the resorts of Sun City, it is very popular with visitors, and accommodation in the private lodges must be booked well in advance.

Staying in the Pilanesberg
Accommodation ranges from the luxurious to cottages and caravan facilities. The top private lodges are:
• **Kwa Maritane:** luxury hotel and time-share complex situated in the hills; duplex cabanas and chalets with private patios.
• **Bakubung:** thatched studio rooms and chalets, built around a hippo pool.
• **Tshukudu:** luxury rest camp set on the crest of a ridge; self-contained chalets.

Pilanesberg Safaris
(Sun City safari desk)
☎ (01455) 21-000

South African National Parks
(central reservations)
☎ (012) 428-9111
🖥 www.parks-sa.co.za
✆ reservations@ parks-sa.co.za

Right: *A game viewing hide at the Pilanesberg Game Reserve.*

See Map E–I2   ★★

THE BLYDE RIVER CANYON

Below the confluence of the **Treur** (sorrow) and **Blyde** (joy) rivers is one of the continent's great natural wonders: a massive and majestic red-sandstone gorge, whose incredible cliff faces plunge almost sheer to the waters below. The gorge is 20km (12 miles) long and has been dammed

to create a picturesque lake; at the top of the canyon there are viewing points easily reached from the main road, from which you can gaze across the Lowveld plain and, closer, at the massifs of the **Mariepskop** and the **Three Rondavels**.

Much of the countryside around the gorge is occupied by the **Blyde River Canyon Nature Reserve**, known for its diverse plant and bird life, which includes the imposing black (Verreaux's) eagle and the rare bald ibis which nests on the granite cliffs. It is also a fine place for ramblers and horseback riders. Within and just outside the reserve are two pleasant resorts, a reptile park and **Bourke's Luck Potholes**, an intriguing fantasia of water-fashioned rocks.

Perhaps the most breathtaking view site on the entire **Escarpment** is the aptly named **God's Window**, a gap in the high mountain rampart near the southern extremity of the Blyde River Canyon Nature Reserve.

Above: *Part of the Blyde River Canyon Nature Reserve, a magnificent upland sanctuary fringing the famed Blyde River Canyon.*

Blyde River Canyon Nature Reserve
☎ (013) 769-6031

Bourke's Luck Information Centre
☎ (013) 769-6019

Mpumalanga Tourism Authority
☎ /📠 (013) 752-7001

South African National Parks
(central reservations)
☎ (012) 428-9111
🖥 www.parks-sa.co.za
📧 reservations@parks-sa.co.za

Above: *Crystal-clear paddling pools on Durban's Golden Mile.*

⭐ *See* Map K ★★

KWAZULU-NATAL COAST

Known as the 'garden province', KwaZulu-Natal is a land of rolling green hills and a magnificent **Indian Ocean** coastline stretching some 600km (370 miles) from Mozambique in the north to the Umtamvuna River in the south, with much of the region's northern half occupied by historic **Zululand**.

Durban is the country's third largest city, and its foremost seaport (the harbour is Africa's biggest and busiest and is ranked ninth in the world). The city sprawls along the coast to the south, across the Umgeni River in the north, and up and beyond the Berea, a ridge of hills that overlooks the city, the beachfront and the bay.

Durban and its subtropical surrounds are among the southern hemisphere's best-known holiday playgrounds, popular for its beaches, restaurants, hotels, nightspots, shopping complexes, museums, galleries, parks and gardens, and sport amenities. But Durban's true attractions lie along the seafront: the **Victoria Embankment**, the **Port Natal Maritime Museum** and the **Golden Mile**.

The upmarket resort area of **Umhlanga Rocks** on Durban's **North Coast** boasts fine beaches, luxury hotels, holiday homes and apartments, excellent shops, and more than 30 restaurants, while the **South Coast** lays claim to the bustling resort town of **Amanzimtoti** and the nearby **Amanzimtoti Bird Sanctuary**.

Durban International Airport
☎ (031) 451-6666

Durban Unlimited
✉ Tourist Junction, Old Station Building, Pine Street, Durban
☎ (031) 304-4934
📠 (031) 304-3868

Tourism KwaZulu-Natal
☎ (033) 845-1002
✉ see above
☎ (031) 304-7144
📠 (031) 304-8792
💻 www.tourism-kzn.org

Natal Sharks Board
☎ (031) 566-0400

Wildlife and Environment Society
☎ (031) 201-3126

KwaZulu-Natal Coast & St Lucia

🌼 *See* Map E–J3　　★ ★

GREATER ST LUCIA WETLAND PARK

From the St Lucia Park north to **Sodwana Bay** and inland, incorporating Lake St Lucia, is an area comprising an intricate mix of lakes and lagoons, pans, marshland and swamps, sandy forests, palm veld and grassland as well as dunes, beaches and offshore coral reefs – collectively known as Greater St Lucia Wetland Park. The centrepiece of this huge conservation area is **Lake St Lucia**, an extensive, shallow estuarine system that teems with water-birds, and is home to crocodile and hippo. Among the wildlife wonders of the world, gravid sea turtles – loggerheads and leatherbacks – come ashore to lay their eggs on the beaches.

Among visitor amenities are walking trails and excellent opportunities for game-viewing, bird-watching, boating, fishing, scuba diving and snorkelling. Don't miss the *Santa Lucia* boat tour, which ferries visitors the length of the estuary. The wetland park, a conservation area that gained international recognition as a **World Heritage Site** status in 2000, is part of a much grander scheme – the **Lubombo Spacial Development Initiative** – which takes in other regional conservation areas, together with parts of **Swaziland** and parts of southern **Mozambique**.

**KwaZulu-Natal
Nature Conservation**
✉ Pietermaritzburg
☎ (033) 845-1002

**South African
National Parks**
(central reservations)
☎ (012) 428-9111
💻 www.parks-sa.co.za
🖰 reservations@
parks-sa.co.za

**Tourism
KwaZulu-Natal**
☎ (033) 845-1002
✉ Tourist Junction,
Old Station Building,
Pine Street, Durban
☎ (031) 304-7144
📠 (031) 304-8792
💻 www.
tourism-kzn.org

**Wildlife and
Environment Society**
☎ (031) 201-3126

Below: *The Greater St Lucia Wetland Park is today a World Heritage Site.*

HIGHLIGHTS

Battlefields Route
☎ (082) 802-1643

KwaZulu-Natal Nature Conservation
☎ (033) 845-1002

Midlands Meander
☎ (0333) 36-008

Pietermaritzburg Publicity Association
☎ (033) 345-1348

Tourism KwaZulu-Natal
✉ Old Station Building, Pine Street, Durban
☎ (031) 304-7144
📠 (031) 304-8792
🖥 www.tourism-kzn.org

Zululand Regional Council
☎ (035) 870-0812

Below: *Pietermaritzburg's City Hall, with its stained-glass windows and ornate clock tower, is a fine example of Victorian architectural heritage.*

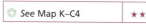

See Map K–C4   ★★

KWAZULU-NATAL MIDLANDS

Inland, the KwaZulu-Natal countryside rises to the foothills and then to the massive heights of the Great Escarpment, here known as the Drakensberg (or as legend has it, 'dragon mountain').

The province's predominantly rural economy is based on the sugar-cane plantations along its seaboard, but further inland the major commodities include subtropical and tropical fruits (pineapples, bananas), dairy products, timber and maize.

The main town between the coastal strip and the Drakensberg is historic and charming **Pietermaritzburg**, while beyond are the grasslands of the Midlands – home to the Zulu nation and scene of bloody conflicts between Briton, Boer and Zulu.

Pietermaritzburg is a beautiful city of red-brick Victorian buildings, cast-iron store fronts, antique shops, book stores, and of parks and gardens. It was founded by Voortrekkers in 1838, and its origins can be seen in the **Voortrekker Museum**, formerly known as the Church of the Vow, a

small, gabled edifice erected by the Boers to commemorate their 1838 victory over the Zulus at **Blood River**.

The city's history and character are, however, British colonial rather than Afrikaner; its Victorian heritage on display throughout the enclave.

VALLEY OF A THOUSAND HILLS

The most striking feature of the KwaZulu-Natal Midlands is the valley of the **Umgeni River** between the flat-topped sandstone massif of KwaZulu-Natal's **Table Mountain**, and the Indian Ocean to the east. The area is densely populated in some

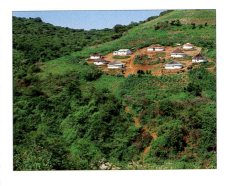

parts, ruggedly wild in others; the vistas are magnificent, the flora (red-hot pokers, Mexican sunflowers, aloes and, especially, a wealth of lilies) a delight to the eye.

The road that leads along the valley's southern rim is lined with farm and craft stalls and tea gardens; there are also craft studios and shops in and around the small centre of **Bothas Hill** (among them Selkirk's Curio Gallery, The Weavers' Studio next door, The Pottery Studio and The Barn Owl). Intriguing African art and craft can be seen, too, in the unusual, vaguely Tudor-style **Rob Roy Hotel**, whose terrace is the venue for carvery lunches and cream teas.

If you're in search of the 'authentic' Africa, stop off at **PheZulu**, a 'living museum' village featuring Zulu domestic life, dancing (a pulsating spectacle), bone-throwing, African cooking, thatching, spear-making, an art gallery and a shop. Nearby **Assagay Safari Park** has Nile crocodiles (100 of them), snakes, a natural history museum, a shop, a restaurant and picnic sites.

Above: *The aptly named Valley of a Thousand Hills lies between Durban and Pietermaritzburg.*

Assagay Safari Park
☎ (031) 777-1000

South African National Parks
(central reservations)
☎ (012) 428-9111
🖥 www.parks-sa.co.za
✆ reservations@parks-sa.co.za

Tourism KwaZulu-Natal
✉ Tourist Junction, Old Station Building, Pine Street, Durban
☎ (031) 304-7144
📠 (031) 304-8792
🖥 www.tourism-kzn.org

Above: *The Hole-in-the-Wall is pounded by waves.*

East London
Tourism Information
☎ (043) 722-6015

Cwebe Nature
Reserve
☎ (041) 390-2179

Sun International
(central reservations)
☎ (011) 780-7800

Tourism
Port Elizabeth
✉ Donkin Lighthouse,
Donkin Reserve
☎ (041) 585-8884

Wild Coast Holiday
Reservations
☎ (043) 743-6181

See Map E–H5 ★★

WILD COAST

Northwards along the Eastern Cape coast lies the river port of East London, and beyond that the rugged shore known as the Wild Coast. It is an unspoilt wilderness of beaches and bays, lagoons and estuaries (an impressive 18 rivers find their way to the ocean along here), cliffs and rocky reefs that probe out to sea. Rolling green hills and patches of dense vegetation grace the hinterland.

The **Wild Coast Sun** resort complex is a prime tourist destination. A wide range of water sports, a golf course, gaming rooms, restaurants, a theatre and two lively show bars are just some of the visitor amenities. Other hotels in quaint towns and hamlets along this coast are more suitable for the leisure-bent visitor: rock, deep-sea, surf and lagoon angling; swimming, surfing, diving (there are sharks!), or just revelling in the unspoilt surroundings, are some options.

The seaboard's most distinctive physical feature is the **Hole-in-the-Wall**: a massive, detached cliff, with an arched opening through which the surf thunders – an hour-and-a-half's walk south along the coast from **Coffee Bay**. Coastal conservation areas are the small adjoining **Dwesa** and **Cwebe** nature reserves, whose attractions include birds, rivers, forest and a waterfall.

See Map F–A1   ★ ★

THE CAPE WEST COAST

While Cape Town, or the Mother City as it is affectionately known, is considered the Western Cape's premier travel destination, there is much to see and enjoy beyond the confines of the city. Inland are the grand mountain ranges and fertile valleys of the Winelands (*see* page 21), and to the north Namaqualand (*see* page 33), which is transformed in spring with vast fields of brightly coloured wildflowers. In between is the rugged and windswept West Coast, which has a beauty of its own.

A pleasant excursion is that leading up the west coast to **Langebaan Lagoon**, one of the country's finest wetlands and a birdwatcher's paradise. Visit the **West Coast National Park** (headquarters at Langebaan Lodge) and Langebaan village (boat trips, country club, **Club Mykonos** – a Greek-style entertainment and time-share complex). On the northern side of the lagoon, the tiny village of **Paternoster**, a popular crayfishing spot, is not far away from **Saldanha Bay** (mussels, crayfishing and boat trips).

Cape Town Tourism Visitor's Centre
✉ Burg Street, Cape Town
☎ (021) 426-4260

MTN Flowerline
☎ (083) 910-1028

MTN Whale Hotline
☎ (073) 214-6949

South African National Parks
(central reservations)
☎ (012) 428-9111
🖥 www.parks-sa.co.za
🖰 reservations@parks-sa.co.za

West Coast Tourism
☎ (022) 433-2380
🖷 (022) 433-2172

Below: *The Greek-style village resort, Club Mykonos.*

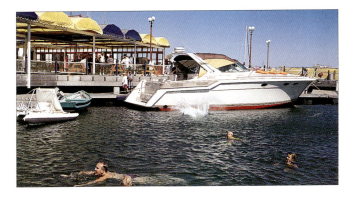

Gauteng Tourism
✉ Rosebank Mall,
Rosebank,
Johannesburg
☎ (011) 327-2000

Satour
(national tourism body)
☎ (011) 778-8000

Indula Safaris & Tours
☎ (012) 811-0197

Sakabula Safaris & Tours
☎ (083) 460-3097

Pretoria Information Centre
✉ Church Square
☎ (012) 337-4487

Below: *In spring, Pretoria becomes a haze of exquisite lilac, thanks to the blossoms of the city's many jacaranda trees.*

❀ *See* Map B	★

PRETORIA

The administrative capital of South Africa, Pretoria was recently renamed Tshwane, but is still commonly referred to by the name it has held since the 1800s. The city is noted for its historic buildings, parks and flora. Some 70,000 purple-flowered jacaranda trees line the city's streets – hence the informal name of 'Jacaranda City'.

Pretoria's industry includes engineering, food processing and diamond mining (the 3025-carat Cullinan Diamond – the world's biggest – was unearthed here in 1905).

The city is also a research and learning centre – Pretoria University; Unisa, the world's largest correspondence university; Onderstepoort, a renowned veterinary research institute; Medunsa, the Medical University of South Africa; Vista University; the Council for Scientific and Industrial Research (CSIR); the Human Sciences Research Council (HSRC); and the South African Bureau of Standards (SABS).

Pretoria is also the headquarters of the **South African National Parks Board**, the parastatal organization that manages the country's wildlife areas, including the Kruger National Park. The city is, however, perhaps better known for its charming **Church Square**, the majestic **State Theatre** and the **National Zoological Gardens**.

See Map E–I2
★

PILGRIM'S REST

When gold was found on the Escarpment in 1873, diggers flocked in, setting up camps at Spitzkop and MacMac and later – after an even richer strike – at Pilgrim's Rest, so named because, after many false trails, the gold-hunters finally found a home here.

Above: *Victorian homes on Pilgrim's Rest's main street have been very well preserved.*

The tents and shacks were eventually replaced with iron-roofed cottages, traders set up shop, a church and a newspaper appeared, the **Royal Hotel** opened its doors, and for some years the settlement flourished. Eventually, however, the gold ran out and syndicates were formed to dig deeper. The last of the mines closed in the 1970s, although long before then (1940s) owners had spread their investments, diversifying into timber. Some of the world's largest man-made forests (pine and wattle) now mantle the Escarpment.

Pilgrim's Rest still supports a few hundred residents, and its charming character (1880–1915) has been preserved as a 'living museum'. The Royal Hotel still hosts visitors, and its pub is well patronized. The rooms you sleep in are very much as they were 100 years ago. Also available to guests are some of the miners' cottages, and there are tours of the village, the **Diggers' Museum** (gold-panning demonstrations) and **Alanglade**, the home of an early mine manager.

Mpumalanga Tourism Authority
☎/🖷 (013) 752-7001

Pilgrim's Rest Information Centre
☎ (013) 768-1060

Royal Hotel
✉ Main Road, Pilgrim's Rest
☎ (013) 768-1100
🖷 (013) 768-1188

🌀 *See* Map J–A1 | ★

Above: *Visitors to some of Oudtshoorn's ostrich show farms are able to ride the giant birds.*

Ecobound Tours & Travel
☎ (044) 871-4455 / (083) 700-7907

Flower Route
(Southern Cape Herbarium, George)
☎ (044) 874-9295

Garden Route Tourism
☎ (044) 873-6314/55
📠 (044) 884-0688

Little (Klein) Karoo Wine Route
☎ (044) 279-2532 (Oudtshoorn)
☎ (044) 213-3312 (Calitzdorp)

THE LITTLE KAROO

Contrasting sharply with the lush coast, the Little Karoo, with its harsh beauty, sprawls between the **Outeniqua** and the **Langeberg** mountain ranges and the grand **Swartberg**. The flattish plain below these uplands is part of the Karoo system, but is very different from the Great Karoo that lies beyond the Swartberg. It is not a high rainfall area, but is watered by the many streams that flow from the mountains, and the land yields rich harvests of wheat, lucerne, tobacco, grapes and walnuts.

Oudtshoorn was (and is) the focal point of the ostrich industry, which had its heyday during the ostrich-feather boom in the late 19th and early 20th centuries. The reminders of this can be seen in the 'feather palaces', built by the wealthy farmers.

Visit the annex of the **C.P. Nel Museum** for its Ostrich Room and antiques. Other surviving mansions include **Dorphuis**, **Pinehurst** and, outside town, **Greystones** and **Welgeluk**. Among the ostrich show-farms are the worthwhile **Highgate** and **Safari**. Both offer guided tours during which you are shown all facets of the ostrich business, and are given the opportunity to watch the birds going through their paces on the racetrack (in the 'ostrich derbys').

Just to the north of the town is one of the region's most visited tourist attractions: the labyrinthine caverns of the **Cango Caves**.

See Map E–C4   ★

NAMAQUALAND

At first sight the plains of Namaqualand, the arid western coastal strip stretching up to the Orange (Gariep) River and Namibia in the north, seems too harsh and inhospitable to support any but the hardiest kinds of life. Yet the region is unbelievably rich in succulents and flowering annuals. After the winter rains – late July to September – the land is briefly mantled by carpets of wild flowers.

Namaqualand is home to about 4000 floral species, most of which belong to the daisy and mesembryanthemum (known as *vygies*) groups but there are also aloes, lilies, perennial herbs and a host of others. The small, low-growing plants are drought resistant, the seeds lying dormant during the long dry months. Then, after the winter rains but before the onset of the burning desert winds – when they sense the impending arrival of pollinators – they burst to life, maturing in a matter of days to magically transform the countryside.

It's worth making the long journey to witness the spectacle. Organized tours are available; Specialized Tours, for instance, offer a day trip that embraces **Langebaan Lagoon**, **Mamre** as well as **Darling**; en route you're treated to a seafood lunch and, of course, to marvellous displays of wild flowers. For those who have time on their hands, a longer three-day tour is recommended.

Flower Times
The best months are Aug–Sep, but varies from year to year. Call the Flowerline first.
• The best displays are in the Postberg Nature Reserve, Clanwilliam, the Biedouw Valley, Vanrhynsdorp, Nieuwoudtville, Kamieskroon and Springbok.
• On sunny days flowers open between 10:00 and 16:30; on overcast days they do not open at all.
• A flower tour can be done in one day, but allow two to three days for the major routes.
• Take warm clothing, as the mornings and evenings can still be very chilly in spring.

MTN Flowerline
☎ (083) 910-1028

Namaqualand Information Bureau
☎ (0251) 22-011

Below: *The colourful springtime glory of Namaqualand.*

The Silent Chambers of Sterkfontein

To the northwest of Pretoria, in the famed Sterkfontein caves, Dr Robert Broom's archaeological excavations yielded a million-year-old fossilized cranium of ape-man *Australopithecus africanus*. The cathedral-like chambers and underground lake are fascinating. Sterkfontein and its neighbouring cave complexes were recently declared a World Heritage Site.

Historic Buildings

Union Buildings, Pretoria

The neoclassical buildings, designed by Sir Herbert Baker, were completed in 1913. The landscaped grounds are open to the public. Of note are the amphitheatre, the Garden of Remembrance and Delville Wood memorial.

✉ *Church Street, Meintjieskop,*
☎ *(012) 325-2000.*

Church Square, Pretoria

Pretoria developed around Church Square, the marketplace and focal point of the isolated Boers' *nagmaal* (communion), baptisms and weddings. Prominent here are the Old Raadsaal (parliament), in French Renaissance style and completed in 1889, and the Palace of Justice. The square's most striking feature is Anton van Wouw's bronze of Paul Kruger.

✉ *Corner Church and Paul Kruger streets.*

Voortrekker Monument, Pretoria

The Monument commemorating the Great Trek consists of a massive block ringed by 64 granite ox-wagons; one of the two decorated chambers bears an inscription commemorating the Boer victory over the Zulus at Blood River in 1838. An impressive monument, but it fits awkwardly into the new South Africa.

✉ *Eeufees Road,*
☎ *(012) 326-6770,*
🕑 *09:00–16:45, daily.*

Tuynhuys, Cape Town

The Colonial Regency style Tuynhuys was once a pleasure lodge and is now the office of the president. Note the equestrian statue of Louis Botha, guerrilla leader during the Anglo-Boer War (1899–1902) and prime minister from 1910–19, that stands on the Plein Street side.

✉ *Parliament Street,*
☎ *(021) 464-2100,*
📠 *(021) 464-2217.*

Houses of Parliament, Cape Town

The Houses of Parliament, built in 1884 on Government Avenue, are recognized as an architectural masterpiece. The gallery is open to the public during parliamentary sessions (Jan–Jun); tickets are available from Room 12.

✉ *Parliament Street,*
☎ *(021) 403-2911,*
🚌 *guided tours Mon–Fri, Jul–Jan.*

The Castle of Good Hope, Cape Town

The Castle, the oldest occupied building in South Africa, is a huge pentagonal fortress built to defend the Dutch colony in 1676. It serves primarily as a museum and exhibits furniture, carpets, *objets d'art* and the paintings of the William Fehr Collection.

✉ *Corner Darling and Buitenkant streets,*
☎ *(021) 469-1111,*
🕐 *09:00–16:00,*
🚌 *10:00–15:00 (hourly), daily.*

Rhodes Memorial, Cape Town

This tribute to 19th-century financier, statesman and visionary **Cecil John Rhodes**, situated on the eastern slopes of Devil's Peak, was designed in grandly classical style as a 'temple' by the celebrated British architect Herbert Baker. Rudyard Kipling's farewell words to the 'immense and brooding spirit' are inscribed on a bust of Rhodes. G.F. Watts' statue, *Physical Energy*, is part of the complex and there is also a restaurant.

✉ *Groote Schuur Estate,*
🕐 *08:00–18:00 May–Sep, 07:30–19:00 Oct–Apr.*

Above: *The stately Houses of Parliament on Cape Town's Government Avenue.*

City of Gold
While Johannesburg has more than its fair share of significant buildings that relate the story of its development, few are more telling than mountainous mine dumps and the rusting headgear of the old gold mines that survive as a reminder of the heady days of when Johannesburg (know to the Zulu people as *eGoli*, the 'city of gold') was more of a digger's camp than a city. The industry has now moved outwards to exploit the still immense wealth of the East and West Rand and the Free State.

Below: *Johannesburg Art Gallery houses a number of impressive paintings.*

Museums and Galleries
MuseuMAfricA, Johannesburg
A treasure house of geological specimens, paintings, prints and photographs relating to the history of South Africa, notably the dark apartheid years.
⊠ *Market Theatre Complex, Mary Fitzgerald Square,*
☎ *(011) 833-5624,*
🕘 *09:00–17:00, daily.*

Johannesburg Art Gallery
Impressive array of permanent displays and temporary exhibitions, as well as a sculptural park.
⊠ *Klein Street, Joubert Park,*
☎ *(011) 725-3130,*
🕘 *10:00–17:00, daily.*

Transvaal Museum, Pretoria
This was once the headquarters of Robert Broom and other celebrated archaeologists. Most notable of the varied displays are those of the man-apes, the bird hall, and the 'Life's Genesis' expo.
⊠ *Paul Kruger Street,*
☎ *(012) 322-7632,*
🕘 *09:00–17:00 Mon– Sat, 11:00–17:00 Sun,*
💻 *www.nfi.co.za/ tmpage.html*
💰 *R8, children R5.*

Melrose House, Pretoria
This elegant 19th-century home in pretty gardens is where the British Commander, Lord Kitchener stayed during the South African (Anglo-Boer) War (1899–1902). It is here that the Treaty of Vereeniging, which ended the war, was signed in May 1902.
⊠ *275 Jacob Mare Street,*
☎ *(012) 322-2805,*
🕘 *10:00–17:00, Tues–Sun.*

Local History Museum, Durban

Durban's Local History Museum is one of the most highly regarded period museums in the country, and offers an intriguing insight into KwaZulu-Natal.

✉ *Corner of Smith and Aliwal streets,*
☎ *(031) 300-6241,*
🕐 *08:30–17:00 Mon–Sat, 11:30–17:00 Sun.*

Durban Art Gallery

Boasting one of the finest collections of indigenous art in the country, the gallery was the first in South Africa to collect and display local black art in the 1970s.

✉ *City Hall, Francis Farewell Square,*
☎ *(031) 300-6234,*
🕐 *08:30–16:00 Mon–Sat, 11:00–16:00 Sun.*

Talana Museum

In commemoration of the start of the Anglo-Boer War in 1899, with tours along the Battlefields Route to the many battle sites.

✉ *Dundee,*
☎ *(0341) 22-677.*

Cultural History Museum, Cape Town

Originally the local slave lodge and brothel, the South African Cultural History Museum looks at the many people of the Cape Colony. The museum houses thematic displays and a wealth of Oriental and other *objets d'art.*

✉ *Corner of Adderley and Wale Streets,*
☎ *(021) 460-8240,*
🕐 *08:30–16:30 Mon–Fri, 09:00–13:00 Sat,*
🖥 *www.museums.org.za/sachm/osl/*
💰 *R7, children R2.*

Bo-Kaap Museum

This fascinating little 1760s period house is Cape Town's oldest surviving town residence. Furnishings are typical of an 18th-century Muslim home.

✉ *71 Wale Street,*
☎ *(021) 481-3939,*
📠 *(021) 481-3938,*
🕐 *09:30–16:00 Mon–Sat, closed Sun and Eid holidays,*
💰 *adults R5, scholars R2, under-6 free.*

Above: *The exhibits of the Old Slave Lodge today form part of the South African Cultural History Museum.*

The Pick of Cape Town's Best Museums
Koopmans-De Wet House on Strand Street: yellowwood and stinkwood furniture, including 'riempie stools'.
Michaelis Collection (Old Town House) on Greenmarket Square: 17th-century Dutch and Flemish paintings.
Natale Labia Museum in Muizenberg: works of art and fine furniture.
Rhodes Cottage, between Muizenberg and St James: Cecil Rhodes' last home.
Simon's Town Naval Museum: interesting collection of naval and local history exhibits.

Highlights of the Parks and Reserves

For information on other parks and reserves, turn to the following pages:
• **Kruger** (page 17)
• **Royal Natal National Park** (page 18)
• **Pilanesberg Game Reserve** (page 22)
• **Blyde River Canyon Reserve** (page 23)
• **St Lucia** (page 25)

Cape Peninsula National Park

The entire Cape Peninsula, stretching from Signal Hill to Cape Point and including Table Mountain and the Cape of Good Hope Nature Reserve, was declared a national park in May 1998. The new park covers about 30,000ha (74,000 acres) of state and private land, and includes thousands of animal and plant species – including fynbos.
☎ (021) 701-8692.

Below: *The magnificent Hluhluwe-Umfolozi Park.*

Parks and Reserves

National Zoological Gardens, Pretoria

This, the largest of Africa's zoological gardens, is home to an array of African and exotic animals, such as the four great apes, the rare South American maned wolf, a white tiger, and a giant eland. A cableway takes visitors to the summit of a hill, from where they view wildlife. The zoo also contains 200 bird species, and there's an aquarium and reptile park.
✉ *Corner of Paul Kruger and Boom streets,*
☎ *(012) 328-3265,*
🕐 *08:00–17:30 May–Aug, 08:00–17:00 Sept–Apr.*

De Wildt Cheetah Station

This breeding and research centre 30km (19 miles) west of Pretoria provides a fine experience for wildlife enthusiasts, and has been widely acclaimed for its successful programme.
✉ *Brits,*
🕐 *08:00–14:15, daily.*

Hluhluwe-Umfolozi Park

This is the most prominent reserve in Maputaland – a magnificent area of woodland savanna and floodplain. Once two separate parks, it is now a haven for the Big Five, as well as cheetah, giraffe, zebra and wild dog. The park is best known for its rhino conservation programme, Operation Rhino, established in the 1960s.
✉ *30km (18 miles) west of Ulundi,*
☎ *(0331) 845-1000,*
🕐 *06:00–18:00 Apr–Sept, 05:00–19:00 Oct–Mar.*

Phinda Resource Reserve

This private reserve bordering Mkuzi is one of the most up-market in the country. Home to cheetah and four of the Big Five, it has a private lodge in the Ubombo range, and a rock lodge and forest lodge, which is set in the heart of its riverine forest.
✉ *80km (50 miles) from Empangeni,*
☎ *(011) 784-7077,*
🕐 *restricted access.*

Addo Elephant National Park

Addo was proclaimed to preserve the remnants of the once prolific Cape elephant population, which had been reduced to no more than 11. Today, that number is more than 200, but the park is also a sanctuary for rhino, buffalo, eland and 170 bird species. Good roads and view points.
✉ *72km (45 miles) from Port Elizabeth,*
☎ *(042) 233-0556,*
🕐 *07:00–19:00, daily.*

Tsitsikamma National Park

The park embraces an 80km (50 mile) strip of coastline, with a marine reserve that streches 5km (3 miles) offshore, with an Underwater Trail. The land is richly endowed with plants and birds, rock pools with plenty of marine life, and whales and dolphins can be seen offshore. Indigenous trees of the forest reserve include giant yellow-woods. There is also the Otter Trail, from the Storms River to Nature's Valley (book well in advance).
✉ *Keurboomstrand, 14km (8 miles) east of Plettenberg Bay,*
☎ *(042) 35-1180,*
🕐 *05:30–21:30, daily.*

Above: *The densely vegetated Addo is able to support an elephant population three times denser than any other reserve in Africa.*

Private Game Reserves
Idube
☎ (013) 735-5459
📠 (013) 735-5432
Inyati
☎ (013) 735-5125
📠 (013) 735-5032
Londolozi
☎ (013) 735-5653
📠 (013) 735-5100
Mala Mala
☎ (013) 735-5661
📠 (013) 735-5686
Ngala
☎ (015) 793-1453
📠 (015) 793-1555
Sabi Sabi
☎ (013) 735-5656
📠 (013) 735-5165
Singita
☎ (013) 735-5456
📠 (013) 735-5746
Ulusaba
☎ (013) 735-5546
📠 (013) 735-5171

<u>Peace and Quiet</u>
- **Bluff Nature Reserve** in Jacobs: one of Durban's best bird-watching spots.
- **Beachwood Mangroves Nature Reserve**, north of Durban: one of the area's last surviving mangrove swamps.
- **Krantzkloof Nature Reserve**: a place of deep gorges, streams, waterfalls and forest; features rare plant and bird species.
- **Umgeni River Bird Park**: rated third among the world's top bird parks, with over 400 exotic and local species in huge, walk-through aviaries.

Below: *The proteas are a common feature on the colourful landscape of Kirstenbosch.*

Botanical Gardens

Johannesburg Botanical Gardens

This welcome retreat from the bustle of South Africa's biggest metropolis is tucked away in Emmarentia. Particularly striking in springtime, and is best noted for its herb and rose gardens.
✉ *Emmarentia,*
☎ *(011) 784-7077,*
🕓 *all hours.*

Durban Botanical Gardens

Established as an experimental station for tropical crops, these gardens boast indigenous flora, an orchid house, and a garden for the blind.
✉ *Sydenham Road,*
☎ *(031) 21-3022,*
🕓 *07:30–17:30, daily.*

Donkin Reserve, Port Elizabeth

Sitting atop a hill overlooking the city, the park-like reserve is encircled by buildings and encloses a number of monuments and memorials.
✉ *Belmont Terrace,*
☎ *(041) 55-8884,*
🕓 *08:30–16:30 Mon–Fri, 09:30–15:30 Sat–Sun.*

Kirstenbosch National Botanical Garden

One of the world's most celebrated botanical gardens. About a quarter of southern Africa's 24,000 species are grown here: proteas, ferns, ericas and more. Walk through the herb and fragrance gardens, the cycad amphitheatre, and the new Visitor's Centre. Summer concerts are held on the lawns.
✉ *Rhodes Avenue,*
☎ *(021) 762-9120,*
🕓 *08:00–18:00 Apr–Aug, 08:00–19:00 Sep–Mar,*
🚌 *10:00–18:00, hourly.*

ACTIVITIES

The country's climate and location make it ideal for sport and leisure activities and it has thus become famous for the variety of adventures it can offer its ever-growing number of visitors.

South Africa's long coastline presents a striking study in contrasts. The western seaboard's rocky wind-blown shoreline is backed by raised beaches that stretch inland for up to 50km (31 miles). It is washed by the cold **Benguela Current**, and boasts a wealth of seabirds (colonies of gannets, cormorants and terns roost and nest on the offshore islands), charming fishing villages, and, for a few brief springtime weeks, a countryside magically transformed by great carpets of wild flowers that attract enthusiasts from far and wide.

The south and east coasts are washed by the warmer waters of the **Agulhas Current**, and in tourist terms are even more popular, attracting hikers, horseriders, fishermen, surfers and other water-sport enthusiasts.

In the south, the 220km (135-mile) **Garden Route** (see page 19), stretching roughly from Heidelberg to the Storms River, is very beautiful; its forested coastal terrace is overlooked by the not-too-distant Outeniqua mountains.

Equally enticing to holiday-makers are the wide expanses of golden sand and the sun-drenched resorts to either side of **Durban** on the east coast.

Above: *The waters of the Mkambati Nature Reserve in the Eastern Cape are a fishing paradise.*

Cape Town Tourism Visitor's Centre
☎ (021) 426-4260

Gauteng Tourism
☎ (011) 327-2000

Satour
(national tourism body)
☎ (011) 778-8000

Garden Route Tourism
☎ (044) 873-6314/55
📠 (044) 884-0688

Winelands Regional Tourism
☎ (021) 872-0686
📠 (021) 872-0534

Tourism KwaZulu-Natal
☎ (033) 845-1002
☎ (031) 304-7144
📠 (031) 304-8792
🖥 www.
tourism-kzn.org

Above: *Sea Point promenade is popular among joggers.*

South African Rugby Football Union
☎ (021) 659-6900

United Cricket Board
☎ (011) 880-2810

Premier Soccer League
☎ (011) 402-2424

Department of Sport and Recreation
☎ (021) 465-7613
📠 (021) 461-4194

Sport Sciences Institute of South Africa
☎ (021) 659-5680
📠 (021) 659-5701

Sport and Recreation

South Africa's wonderfully sunny climate is perfect for outdoor life; its people are enthusiastic and, many of them, accomplished sportspersons.

Soccer is king in the African communities, with around 15,000 clubs and nearly a million regular players. Among the leading professional clubs are Kaizer Chiefs, Orlando Pirates, Mamelodi Sundowns, Jomo Cosmos and Moroka Swallows (all in the Johannesburg–Pretoria area), AmaZulu in KwaZulu-Natal and Santos, Hellenic and Ajax Cape Town in the Western Cape.

Rugby is almost an obsession among many South Africans, and in 1995 the national side (the Springboks) won the coveted Rugby World Cup on its home ground at Ellis Park in Johannesburg.

South Africans, too, are passionate about **cricket** which, as the result of an imaginative development programme, is becoming increasingly popular among people of colour. South Africa hosted the Cricket World Cup in 2003.

Hiking (*see* page 47) and **cycling** are sociable and popular recreations. South Africa's more than 400 **golf** clubs welcome visitors, green fees are reasonable, and most courses are immaculately maintained.

Track and field **athletics** are also gaining a large following, with sterling performances by South Africans in international events. Long-distance **road running** is a popular pastime and quite competitive, the major event being the Two Oceans Marathon in Cape Town, held over Easter each year (with 12,000-plus entrants); a number of world-class runners have already emerged.

The government continues to encourage sponsors to invest in new infrastructure for world-class sporting events.

A growing trend in South Africa, and indeed much of Africa, is the move toward **adventure sports**: caving, bungee-jumping, river rafting, diving with sharks and other adrenaline-pumping activities reserved largely for the brave. Naturally, of course, the country's rugged terrain and abundance of wild, open spaces cater perfectly for this.

River Rafting

A popular way to enjoy the beauty and excitement of South Africa's rivers is to join a group of rafters or canoeists. For most of the river runs, no experience is necessary as experts are at hand to show you the ropes and ensure your safety and comfort. Trips of between one and four days negotiate stretches of the following major watercourses:

• **Orange (Gariep) River**, which runs through the Northern Cape and along the southern border of Namibia.

• **Breede River** near Swellendam in the Western Cape (one operator includes a wine-tasting session on the itinerary!).

• **Thukela River**, which flows over some challenging rapids in central KwaZulu-Natal.

• **Sabie River** in lovely Mpumalanga (rafting here is subject to the seasonal rains).

It is best to join a party organized by a reputable operator, such as:

Felix Unite River Adventures
☎ (021) 670-1300

River Rafters
☎ (021) 712-5094

Left: *Table Bay features prominently on the international sailing calendar.*

Satour
☎ (011) 778-8000

**South African
National Parks**
(central reservations)
☎ (012) 428-9111
🖥 www.parks-sa.co.za
✆ reservations@
parks-sa.co.za

Kruger National Park
☎ (013) 735-4030

**Mpumalanga
Tourism Authority**
☎ /✆ (013) 752-7001

**Tourism
KwaZulu-Natal**
☎ (031) 304-7144
✆ (031) 304-8792
🖥 www.
tourism-kzn.org

**Wildlife and
Environment Society**
☎ (031) 201-3126

BirdLife SA
☎ (011) 789-1122
🖥 www.birdlife.org.za

Below: *Game-
viewing is a popular
pastime in KwaZulu-
Natal's reserves.*

Game-viewing

South Africa's prime tourist attraction and one of its most popular leisure activities – even among locals – is without doubt game-viewing. The country's magnificent wildlife heritage, seen at its most spectacular in the big-game areas of **Mpumalanga** and **KwaZulu-Natal**, which are particularly well frequented by international visitors. In terms of overall species diversity, South Africa ranks third in the world, bested only by Indonesia and the Amazonian forests.

There are more than 20 national parks (a few are very new and still under development) and about 300 smaller regional and local reserves in South Africa, some created primarily to protect wild animals, others the unique plant life or distinctive scenic character of a region. The largest and best known of these is the **Kruger National Park** (*see page 17*), where the great diversity of wildlife includes the Big Five. In addition to the many tourist camps in the park, there is a choice of luxurious lodges in the private reserves along its western boundary. Impressive, too, are the reserves of northern KwaZulu-Natal, which provide habitats for animals and birds.

Quite different in character but just as attractive is **Kgala-gadi Transfrontier Park**, a wilderness of Kalahari dune, sandy plain, thornbush and grassland home to cheetah, lion, wild dog and herds of antelope. Its two segments – one in northern South Africa and the other in southern Botswana – were recently combined to create Africa's first cross-border or 'peace' park, the first of a number of similar such proposals designed to protect Africa's wildlife heritage.

Bird-watching is popular throughout the country, particularly in game-viewing areas such as Mpumalanga and Limpopo, and most of the established parks and reserves boast viewpoints and hides. Kruger alone lays claim to 500 different species of birds, but the urban areas (such as those of Gauteng, KwaZulu-Natal and Cape Town) also have more than their fair share of bird life. More than 300 species have, for example, been identified in the Cape Town area, including sugarbirds, paradise flycatchers, black eagles and a variety of aquatic birds.

It is no surprise, then, that much of the country's hospitality industry is geared to the 'wildlife safari', with almost all the reserves offering a selection of bushveld camps – some fully equipped and serviced – and huts and chalets. Accommodation (*see* pages 54–59) is mostly comfortable, with either private or communal facilities, depending on price.

Above: *Rondavel accommodation at Skukuza, the Kruger National Park's main camp.*

Packing for a Safari

Nobody dresses up in the bush, and most lodges have laundry facilities, which means you could get away with just a few items. Avoid bright colours and white; neutral hues are best for game-viewing and bird-watching. Nights can be chilly, even cold in winter: pack a warm sweater, tracksuit or anorak. You may also need a swimming costume, a sun hat, walking shoes, toiletries that include lip salve and sun-protection cream, good sunglasses, insect repellent, malaria prophylactics, a torch, batteries, binoculars, and bird, mammal, insect, plant and tree field-guides.

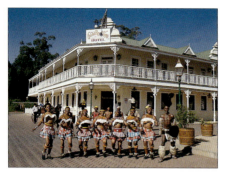

Theme Parks

With sunny skies and a moderate climate, South Africa is an outdoor paradise, which makes it perfect for theme parks and the like, from the historical to the 'just plain fun'. Most are around major urban centres, but there are a number of smaller attractions in the country districts.

An evocative reconstruction of pioneer Johannesburg, **Gold Reef City** (*see* page 14) provides an intriguing look at the history of the City of Gold as the shanty town developed during the gold rush. The buildings are distinctly Victorian in character, as are the beer halls, theatres and even the hotels.

While Durban has its magical **Seaworld** and Port Elizabeth its **Oceanarium and Museum Complex**, Cape Town has the **Two Oceans Aquarium**. On display here is the underwater world of sharks and seals, a 'touch tide pool' (with starfish, sea urchins and much else), a kelp forest, an open ocean tank, a complete coastal ecosystem in miniature (with waterfalls, mountain streams, mudbanks, sand flats and intertidal rock pools), all stocked with appropriate plant, bird and marine life.

Ratanga Junction is very popular over the summer holidays. Fun rides include the Diamond Devil Run, a 'runaway mine train' rollercoaster, Crocodile Gorge, a rapid river ride, and the Bushwacker through the jungle. The prime thrill, however, is the terrifying Cobra rollercoaster!

Gold Reef City
✉ Ormonde, Johannesburg
☎ (011) 496-1600
🕓 09:30–17:00, Tues–Sun
🖥 www.goldreefcity.co.za

Two Oceans Aquarium
✉ Dock Road, V & A Waterfront, Cape Town
☎ (021) 418-3823
📠 (021) 418-3952
🖥 www.aquarium.co.za
🕓 09:30–18:00, daily

Seaworld
✉ West Street, Durban
☎ (031) 337-3526
🕓 09:00–21:00, daily

Port Elizabeth Oceanarium
✉ Marine Drive
☎ (041) 586-1051
🕓 09:00–17:00, daily

Ratanga Junction
✉ Century City, Cape Town
☎ (086) 120-0300
🕓 09:00–22:00, daily, Nov–Apr

Hiking

Hiking through South Africa's wilderness areas remains one of the most popular pastimes for visitors to the country – and the choice is indeed unlimited, from the rugged bushveld of the northern provinces to the mountain slopes and expansive coastlines of KwaZulu-Natal and the Western Cape.

While some established hikes and trails are indeed gruelling and require some level of fitness, others demand no more than a little stamina. In Gauteng, one of the most rewarding is the **Magaliesberg Hills** to the west of the Johannesburg–Pretoria axis. This ridge has a special woodland beauty. Consider staying at Mount Grace Country House or at Valley Lodge (see page 55), and returning via the Rustenburg Nature Reserve.

Much the same is true of **Magoebaskloof**, just beyond Tzaneen. Vegetation here is tropical, making the wooded heights of Woodbush and the nearby Modjadji cycad forest well worth exploring.

While the **Drakensberg** (see page 18) is the country's top hiking spot, firm favourites remain the **Cederberg** (a stark wilderness of rock formations) and, of course, **Table Mountain**. Some mountain walks and climbs are gentle but others are down-right dangerous. All hiking routes throughout South Africa should be treated with respect. Invest in a good map and guidebook; choose a route well within your physical capability and do not stray from the path.

Exploring on Foot

Visitors are free to walk where they wish in the **Cape of Good Hope Nature Reserve**, though seven routes have been charted. These range from the one-hour Kanonkop Trail on the eastern side to the four-hour (one-way) Good Hope Coastal Walk along the western shore to the wreck of the *Phyllisia*. A map of the trail is available at the reserve's entrance. About 20km (12 miles) of tar and gravel roads are also open to mountain bikers; for information contact Day-trippers:
☎ (021) 511-4766
✆ (021) 511-4768

Opposite: *Gold Reef City provides a look at old Johannesburg.*
Below: *Much of the Cape Peninsula is ideal for rambles, walks and hikes.*

Info Africa
⌨ www.infoafrica.co.za

Satour
☎ (011) 778-8000

Garden Route Tourism
☎ (044) 873-6314/55
📠 (044) 884-0688

Outeniqua Choo Tjoe
☎ (044) 382-6960 /
801-8288

Natal Sharks Board
☎ (034) 566-0400

Cape Town Tourism
☎ (021) 426-4260

MTN Flowerline
☎ (083) 910-1028

Below: *Indigenous
cultures such as that
of the Ndebele have
made South Africa
one of the world's
top destinations.*

Organized Tours

With the continued and steady growth in South Africa's tourism industry, more and more avenues are opening up for visitors, with an ever-expanding selection of adventures, from **coach tours** to **helicopter trips**, **cruises** to **hot-air ballooning**, **elephant-back safaris** to **whale-watching**. For details, contact the regional tourism offices.

Following the emergence of the new democracy, an increasing number of visitors are making apoint of exploring the black townships. These **township tours** provide a fascinating insight into the lives of ordinary South Africans, and the sector is growing rapidly. It is, however, best to select a well-established tour operator, such as those that cover Soweto (*see* page 15).

The attraction of indigenous cultures is, in fact, a focal point of local tourism. Those interested in traditional lifestyles should visit the **Ndebele Village** at Loopspruit, 55km (28 miles) from Pretoria, which depicts the progression of the Ndebele building style. Examples of their homes and costumes can

also be seen at the **Botshabelo Museum and Nature Reserve**, **Mapoch Village** (10km from the Tswaing Crater, 40km north of Pretoria), as well as **Lesedi Cultural Village** south of Hartbeespoort Dam. All offer a fine experience.

For a very different kind of thrill, visit the **Natal Sharks Board**. Their demonstrations include the dissection of a shark, audio-visual presentations and a mini museum. The Board has the largest mould of a great white shark in South Africa. Demonstrations are popular, so book in advance.

Although major cities and towns offer guided **city tours** that focus mostly on the origins of the settlement and its development, taking in the prime attractions. Most are also within easy driving distance of the country's top attractions, details of which are provided by local information services.

A favourite excursion on the Garden Route is the train trip between George and Knysna on the **Outeniqua Choo Tjoe**, a Class 24 narrow-gauge steam engine that crosses the Kaaimans bridge to run through woods, along the shore and over the lagoon.

Above: *Tourists travelling to their lodge by ox-cart.*

Taxi Time

Self-drive options are a popular alternative to packaged tours, and are generally safe. Public transport, however, is not as reliable as it should be, and may not be available. During the later years of apartheid rule, boycotts of bus companies and the inadequacies of rail transport gave rise to one of the fastest growing industries in the country. The need for transport presented an entrepreneurial opportunity and the age of minibus taxis was born. These are cheap, fast and sociable, but their safety record is not reassuring.

Right: *The Victoria Wharf shopping mall in Cape Town's V & A Waterfront.*

Shops

South Africa has a free-market economy, and offers the visitor irresistible bargains, from something in gold and diamond (tax-free) at Johannesburg and Cape Town's top shopping malls famed as 'world-in-one' outlets, to a small curio item from a roadside vendor. The value of the rand leans heavily in the favour of overseas visitors.

The most sought-after purchases include soapstone sculptures from one of the many pavement hawkers, bags, belts and books from flea markets or an ostrich-skin briefcase, crocodile-skin bag, hand-woven rugs, and jewellery from stylish shopping malls. If you are interested in ethnic items, flea markets and curio shops are worth a visit.

On your shopping list you can include woven grass tablemats, ostrich eggs and ostrich feathers, colourful bead necklaces, copperware, ceramics, items made from wool and mohair and African handicrafts.

Shopping hours are generally 08:00–17:00 on weekdays and 08:00–13:00 on Saturdays. Supermarkets and most large shopping centres are also open on Sundays.

Best Buys in the Land of Kruger

Although Mpumalanga is best known for the Kruger National Park and the fine local crafts that emanate from the region, it is also a richly productive farming area. Nelspruit and White River have given rise to a proliferation of colourful wayside stalls selling fresh, seasonal produce as well as interesting curios. Look out for:
• subtropical fruits (mangoes, litchis, pineapples, pawpaws, avocados)
• pecan nuts
• macadamia nuts
• hand-woven rugs
• leather goods
• hand carvings

Shopping Malls

Smal Street Mall

A wide range of goods in one of Johannesburg's most popular pedestrian malls, alive with the colours and sounds of Africa.

✉ *Smal Street, Johannesburg CBD.*

Village Walk

Buzzing with shoppers and lunchtime casuals, this is one of the most imaginative malls in Sandton, itself world renowned for its fine shopping experience. Good food and exciting finds, but prices can be rather steep.

✉ *Sandton, Johannesburg.*

Sandton Square

The even more up-market cousin of adjacent Sandton City specializes in top-of-the range goods. Although items may be beyond the means of ordinary pockets, the quality of designer ware is unsurpassed. The lively Italianate courtyard boasts excellent lunch and dinner venues.

✉ *Sandton, Johannesburg.*

The Pavilion

As a recent addition to Durban's galaxy of malls and shopping centres, the Pavilion is a huge, brightly lit treasure house of boutiques, speciality shops and chain stores.

✉ *Westville, Durban.*

Canal Walk

The biggest and the best Cape Town has to offer, and the place to go for choice of shops, but only if you are up for all the walking! The largest shopping centre in Africa offers a vast choice of shops.

✉ *Century City, Cape Town.*

Victoria Wharf

This prime shopping destination offers everything from curio shops to fashion boutiques, cinemas and restaurants. Nearby, too, is the Clocktower Precinct, a popular stop for city shopping.

✉ *V & A Waterfront, Cape Town.*

Midlands Meander

This scenically enchanting arts-and-crafts route in the Midlands of KwaZulu-Natal has been established north of Howick, between and around the little villages of Nottingham Road and Lidgetton. Along the route, studios and workshops offer weaving, pottery, painting, graphics and art restoration.

The Midlands Meander is one of three routes – the attractions of the Last Outposts and the KwaZulu-Natal Midlands Experience itineraries also beckon the leisurely sightseer. Check open days with the Publicity Association in Howick or Pietermaritzburg.

Howick Publicity Association
☎ (033) 330-5305
📠 (033) 330-8154
🖝 nr@futurenet.org.za

Pietermaritzburg Publicity Association
☎ (033) 345-1348
📠 (033) 394-3535
🖝 ppa@futurenet.org.za

Midlands Meander Association
☎ (033) 263-6008/263-6209/330-8195
📠 (033) 263-6008
🖥 www.midlandsmeander.co.za
🖝 info@midlandsmeander.co.za

Above: *Market Theatre flea market with MuseuMAfricA in the background.*

Markets

Many markets take place over weekends and public holidays, mostly in the suburbs of the bigger cities, although a number of country towns have developed small market economies of their own. At craft markets you'll find a splendid variety of original wares, from yellowwood furniture, hand-blown glass, pottery, basketry and jewellery to carpets, tapestries and trendy clothing.

Market Theatre Complex

Johannesburg's favourite marketplace is a vital drawcard to the bohemian precinct.

✉ *Newtown, Johannesburg.*

Oriental Plaza

Perhaps the most famous of Jo'burg's market complexes, this indoor emporium is filled to the brim with curios, fabrics, herbs, spices and more everyday goods. Lively and colourful, with a flavour of the East. ✉ *Fordsburg, Johannesburg.*

The Workshop Flea Market

Taking plumb position near The Workshop shopping centre is one of Durban's liveliest outdoor markets, competing favourably with sister markets at the Amphitheatre and on the South Plaza of the Exhbition Centre. What it lacks in true bargains is made up with sheer exuberance. ✉ *The Workshop, Durban.*

Mzamba Village Market

Small but very typical of South Africa's less

sophisticated outdoor markets, Mzamba (nearby is the more famous Umtamvuna Nature Reserve) is a true delight: nothing pretentious, just lots of good buys, especially locally produced arts and crafts.
✉ *Port Edward.*

The Blue Shed Art and Craft Market, and the Red Shed Craft Workshop

A wide range of ceramics, jewellery, textiles, basketware, township art and candles are on sale.
✉ *V & A Waterfront, Cape Town.*

Greenmarket Square

In a city famed for its many casual outdoor markets, the one within this cobbled square is considered one of the best. It is a vibrant melting-pot of cultural diversity, bustling with shoppers (both locals and visitors) and bargain-hunters, filled with fleamarket stalls and buskers, and fringed by art dealers, gold and diamond merchants, sushi bars, internet cafés, fashion emporiums and historical buildings.
✉ *Cape Town CBD.*

Green Point Stadium

Although it is not particularly pretty or well organized, the market that skirts the sports stadium on Sundays is very popular with locals, offering a wide variety of goods, from brassware to handcrafted curios, mass-produced toys and beadwork.
✉ *Green Point, Cape Town.*

Below: *Umbrellas shade the busy street-traders on Greenmarket Square.*

Above: *The up-market Sandton Sun Hotel in Johannesburg.*

Central Reservations
Protea Hotels
☎ (0800) 11-9000

Formule 1 Hotels
☎ (011) 807-0750

Holiday Inn
☎ (0800) 11-7711

Sun International
☎ (011) 780-7800

Bed & Breakfasts
☎ (011) 482-2206

South African
National Parks
☎ (012) 428-9111
🖥 www.parks-sa.co.za
✆ reservations@
parks-sa.co.za

WHERE TO STAY

The top **hotels** in South Africa are of a very high standard, and many of the most recently opened compare favourably with those of the world's capitals. A voluntary grading system, covering all types of accommodation, is in operation; ratings range from one to five stars.

Many of the established hotels are controlled by one the large chains, such as Holiday Inn, Marriott or Sheraton; most offer packages, out-of-season, family rates and other inducements.

Visitors also have a wide choice of **guest houses** in and around major urban enclaves, and these are becoming more and more commonplace in even country towns and other small hamlets. (Publications available from bookshops.) Outlying areas are also very well endowed with good **country getaways** – restful little lodges tucked away in the valleys. Most are comfortable, many sophisticated in terms of appointment and cuisine, and all are informal and friendly.

Guest farms are ideal for a healthy family holiday. Stay in the farmhouse or in a chalet or cottage on the property, and take part in the life of the ranch, farm or wine estate.

Increasingly popular **self-catering** options throughout the country are numerous and varied, ranging from basic holiday apartments and cottages to well-appointed, luxurious resort-type chalets.

Bed-and-breakfast accommodation is becoming a popular option, and many South Africans are making their homes available to visitors – a trend that is fast taking hold in black 'townships', where locals offer a fascinating insight into their daily lives.

Gauteng and North-West

JOHANNESBURG

Sandton Sun

(Map D–C3)

Popular, with consistently good service.

✉ Sandton,

☎ (011) 780-5000,

📠 (011) 780-5002.

Rosebank Hotel

(Map D–C3)

Comfortable accommodation in up-market Rosebank.

✉ Rosebank,

☎ (011) 447-2700,

📠 (011) 447-3276.

The Grace

(Map D–C3)

Luxury city living at its finest.

✉ Rosebank,

☎ (011) 280-7200,

📠 (011) 280-7474.

Caesar's Palace

(Map D–C3)

Modern comforts in a grand new setting.

✉ Kempton Park,

☎ (011) 928-1000.

Sunnyside Park

(Map A–C1)

Very comfortable and reasonably priced.

✉ Parktown,

☎ (011) 643-7226,

📠 (011) 642-0019.

City Lodge Sandton

(Map D–C3)

Centrally located and although part of the popular chain, still offers good value.

✉ Sandton,

☎ (011) 444-5300,

📠 (011) 444-5315.

The Cottages

(Map D–C3)

Charming and cosy in quaint surrounds, with the feel of home.

✉ Observatory,

☎ (011) 487-2829,

📠 (011) 487-2404.

Ah Ha Guesthouse

(Map D–C3)

Homestyle comforts with both friendly and efficient service.

✉ Bedfordview,

☎ (011) 616-3702,

📠 (011) 615-3012.

Cooper's Croft

(Map D–B3)

A delightful getaway with all the mod-cons.

✉ Randburg,

☎ (011) 787-2679,

📠 (011) 886-7611.

PRETORIA

Arcadia Hotel

(Map B–C1)

Standard hospitality in the heart of the city.

✉ Pretoria central,

☎ (012) 326-9311,

📠 (012) 326-1067.

Garden Court Holiday Inn

(Map B–B2)

Well-positioned and very comfortable.

✉ Pretoria central,

☎ (012) 342-1444.

La Maison

(Map B–C1)

Very cosy and rather reasonably priced too.

✉ Hatfield,

☎ (012) 430-4341.

MAGALIESBERG

Mount Grace Country House

(Map D–B3)

Ultimate luxury set amid scenic splendour.

✉ Magaliesberg,

☎ (014) 577-1350.

📠 (014) 577-1202.

Valley Lodge

(Map D–B3)

Good, reliable service.

✉ Magaliesberg,

☎ (014) 557-1301.

Limpopo and Mpumalanga

THE ESCARPMENT

Mount Sheba
(Map E–I2)
Luxury hotel and time-share in forest reserve.
✉ near Pilgrim's Rest,
☎ /📠 (013) 768-1241.

Blydepoort
(Map E–I2)
Aventura resort on the edge of the canyon.
✉ Blyde River Canyon,
☎ /📠 (012) 808-5078.

LIMPOPO

Glenshiel Country Lodge
(Map E–I1)
Fine and gracious living amid the rolling hills and meadows.
✉ Magoebaskloof,
☎ (015) 276-4335,
📠 (015) 276-4475.

MPUMALANGA LOWVELD

Cybele Forest Lodge
(Map E–I2)
One of the very best woodland lodges, with beautiful rooms.
✉ White River,
☎ (013) 764-1823.

Farmhouse Country Lodge
(Map E–I2)
Thatched luxury suites with great views.
✉ Between White River and Hazyview,
☎ (013) 737-8780,
📠 (013) 737-8783.

Highgrove House
(Map E–I2)
Colonial farmhouse in a garden setting.
✉ Between White River and Hazyview,
☎ (013) 764-1844.

Casa do Sol
(Map E–I2)
Cobbled walkways, arches and fountains.
✉ Between Hazyview and Sabie,
☎ /📠 (013) 737-8111.

Old Joe's Kaia
(Map E–I2)
1920s homestead with river frontage.
✉ White River,
☎ (013) 751-5059.

Sefapane Lodge
(Map E–I1)
Very comfortable 'beehive' cottages.
✉ Phalaborwa,
☎ (013) 781-7041.

TROUTFISHING LODGES

Bergwaters
(Map E–I2)
Quiet retreat in Elands River valley, with old-fashioned hospitality.
✉ Waterval Boven,
☎ (013) 257-7081.

Critchley Hackle Lodge
(Map E–I2)
Peaceful stone complex on the lake edge.
✉ Dullstroom,
☎ (013) 254-0145,
📠 (013) 254-0262.

Dullstroom Inn
(Map E–I2)
Cosy, with a charming pub and good rates.
✉ Dullstroom,
☎ (013) 254-0071.

Walkerson Country Manor
(Map E–I2)
Thatched stone manor with views over the lake and forest.
✉ Dullstroom,
☎ (013) 254-0246.

KRUGER PARK

For rest-camp accommodation in the park, see SANP, page 54.

KwaZulu-Natal

DURBAN

Royal Hotel
(Map M–A3)
One of the country's
oldest and best.
✉ City centre,
☎ (031) 336-6000.

The Edward
(Map M–C2)
Elegant, with
impeccable service.
✉ Marine Parade,
☎ (031) 337-3681,
📞 (031) 332-1692.

Four Seasons
(Map M–C2)
Splendid seaview
rooms plus sports bar.
✉ Gillespie Street,
☎ (031) 337-3381.

SOUTH COAST

Oribi Gorge Hotel
(Map E–I4)
Old-fashioned value
near the reserve.
✉ near Oribi Gorge,
☎ (039) 687-0253.

The Country Lodge
(Map E–I5)
Pretty, secluded beach
spot in Port Edward.
✉ Palm Beach,
☎ (039) 316-8380.

NORTH COAST

Beverly Hills Sun
(Map K–D4)
Comfortable rooms
overlooking the beach.
✉ Umhlanga Rocks,
☎ (031) 561-2211.
📞 (031) 561-3711.

Oyster Box Hotel
(Map K–D4)
Gracious living in up-
market surrounds.
✉ Umhlanga Rocks,
☎ (031) 561-2233,
📞 (031) 561-4076.

PIETERMARITZBURG AND MIDLANDS

Imperial Hotel
(Map K–C4)
Colonial-style living
at its very finest.
✉ Pietermaritzburg,
☎ (033) 342-6551.

M'sunduzi Lodge
(Map K–C4)
Comfortable B&B with
mini-apartments, pool.
✉ Pietermaritzburg,
☎ (033) 394-4388.

Wartburger Hof
(Map K–C4)
Forest and country for
a laid-back lifestyle.
✉ Wartburg,
☎ /📞 (033) 503-1482.

DRAKENSBERG

Mont-aux-Sources Hotel
(Map K–A3)
Smart and attractive.
✉ Mont-aux-Sources,
☎ (036) 438-6303.

Champagne Castle
(Map K–B3)
Pleasant, old-fashioned.
✉ Champagne Castle,
☎ (036) 468-1063.

Cathedral Peak Hotel
(Map K–B3)
Good family resort in
a great setting.
✉ Winterton,
☎ (036) 488-1888.

Drakensberg Sun
(Map K–B3)
Views of Cathkin Peak.
✉ Winterton,
☎ (036) 468-1000.

Sani Pass Lodge
(Map K–B4)
Warm and welcoming.
✉ Himeville,
☎ (033) 702-1320.

Himeville Arms
(Map K–B4)
Cosy and relaxed.
✉ Himeville,
☎ (033) 702-1305.

Eastern Cape

PORT ELIZABETH

Beach Hotel

(Map L–A2)

Close to Oceanarium and Hobie Beach.

✉ *Humewood,*

☎ /📠 *(041) 583-2161.*

Milbrook House

(Map L–B2)

Attractive Victorian B&B with *en suites.*

✉ *Central,*

☎ *(041) 585-3080,*

📠 *(041) 582-3774.*

GRAHAMSTOWN

The Cock House

(Map E–G6)

Mandela's favourite country house.

✉ *Market Street,*

☎ *(046) 622-7326.*

EAST LONDON

Windsor Cabanas

(Map E–H5)

Mediterranean style, self-catering option.

✉ *Near Orient Street,*

☎ *(046) 743-3433.*

Holiday Inn Garden

(Map E–H5)

Standard service.

✉ *beachfront,*

☎ *(043) 722-7260.*

WILD COAST

Morgan's Bay

(Map E–H5)

Very good beach.

✉ *Wild Coast,*

☎ *(043) 841-1062.*

Wild Coast Sun

(Map E–H5)

Lavish casino complex in tropical setting.

✉ *Wild Coast,*

☎ *(011) 780-7800.*

Fish River Sun

(Map E–G6)

Up-market.

✉ *Ciskei coast,*

☎ *(011) 780-7800.*

Mpekweni Marine

(Map E–G6)

Comfort for families.

✉ *Ciskei coast,*

☎ *(011) 780-7800.*

PARKS / RESERVES

Addo Elephant National Park

(Map E–F6)

Self-catering cottages.

✉ see *SANP, page 54,*

Shamwari Game Reserve

(Map E–G6)

See the Big Five in a luxury private reserve.

☎ *(042) 203-1111.*

The Garden Route

TSITSIKAMMA

Tsitsikamma Village Inn

(Map J–E3)

Set in the foothills, with lovely views.

✉ *Tsitsikamma,*

☎ *(042) 281-1711,*

📠 *(042) 281-1669.*

PLETTENBERG BAY

The Plettenberg

(Map J–D3)

Elegant, with international reputation.

✉ *Plettenberg Bay,*

☎ *(044) 533-2030,*

📠 *(044) 533-2074.*

WILDERNESS

Fairy Knowe Hotel

(Map J–B3)

Thatched, riverside rondavels and rooms in a country setting.

✉ *Wilderness,*

☎ *(044) 877-1100,*

📠 *(044) 877-0364.*

KNYSNA

Yellowwood Lodge

(Map J–C3)

Splendid rooms with fine lagoon views.

✉ *Kynsna ,*

☎ *(044) 382-5906,*

📠 *(044) 382-4230.*

Western Cape

CAPE TOWN

The Mount Nelson
(Map H–A4)
World-renowned elegant luxury in the heart of the city.
✉ 76 Orange Street,
☎ (021) 423-1000,
📠 (021) 424-7472.

Park Inn
(Map H–B2)
Conveniently located and overlooking a charming piazza.
✉ Greenmarket Square,
☎ (021) 423-2050,
📠 (021) 423-2059.

V & A WATERFRONT

Breakwater Lodge
(Map I–A3)
Vibrant setting, good value for money.
☎ (021) 406-1911,
📠 (021) 406-1070.

The Table Bay
(Map I–A1)
Ultimate in five-star luxury and comfort, with awesome views.
✉ V & A Waterfront,
☎ (021) 406-5000,
📠 (021 406-5767.

ATLANTIC SEABOARD

The Bay
(Map G–B2)
Splendid luxury with truly spectacular views over the ocean.
✉ Camps Bay,
☎ (021) 430-4444,
📠 (021) 438-4455.

The Peninsula All-Suite
(Map G–B1)
Overlooking the bay, stunning ocean views.
✉ Sea Point,
☎ (021) 430-7777,
toll-free 0800-224433,
📠 (021) 430-7776.

SOUTHERN SUBURBS

Alphen Hotel
(Map G–C2)
18th-century manor in the Constantia Valley.
✉ Constantia,
☎ (021) 794-5011.

Vineyard Hotel
(Map G–C2)
This hotel is in a historic country house, located in a lovely quiet setting.
✉ Newlands,
☎ (021) 683-3044,
📠 (021) 683-3365.

WINELANDS

D'Ouwe Werf
(Map F–B2)
Small, historic and very charming.
✉ Stellenbosch,
☎ (021) 887-4608,
📠 (021) 887-4626.

Lanzerac Hotel
(Map F–B2)
Gracious, with truly historic atmosphere.
✉ Stellenbosch,
☎ (021) 887-1132,
📠 (021) 887-2310.

Lord Charles Hotel
(Map F–B3)
Arguably one of the best luxury hotels.
✉ Somerset West,
☎ (021) 855-1040,
📠 (021) 855-1107.

Grande Roche
(Map F–C2)
International standard among the vines.
✉ Paarl,
☎ (021) 863-2727,
📠 (021) 863-2220.

Le Ballon Rouge
(Map F–C2)
A stylish and up-market establishment.
✉ Franschhoek,
☎ (021) 876-2651.

Fresh from the Farm
Although South Africa
can suffer long bouts
of debilitating drought
(only 12% of the land
is suitable for arable
farming), it is indeed
one of the world's few
food exporting regions.
A wide range of crops
is grown, from sugar
cane and subtropical
fruits in KwaZulu-Natal
through the maize
harvests of the North
West to the tobacco
in Mpumalanga. The
national cattle herd
numbers about 12
million head while
some 27 million sheep
graze the plains of the
Great Karoo, Free State
and Eastern Cape.

Below: *A traditional
Cape Malay feast.*

EATING OUT
What to Eat

South Africa's special culinary draw cards include the local meat and venison (such as springbok, ostrich, kudu and impala), fruit, fish, shellfish – particularly rock lobster (crayfish) – and other seafood delicacies such as abalone (perlemoen) and oysters. There isn't, however, a single, coherent South African cuisine – the country is too ethnically diverse, and eating patterns are drawn from many different parts of the world. Nevertheless, eating traditions of some immigrant groups – Greek, German, Portuguese, for example – are more prominent than others in various regions. Durban restaurants are renowned for fiery **curries** and *breyanis*; the Cape for traditional fare in which Karoo lamb, venison, sweet potato, cinnamon-flavoured pumpkin and sweet *konfyt* are popular. The Cape, too, is the home of **Malay cuisine**, noted for its fragrant *bredies* (a mutton stew with potato,

onion and other vegetables), as well as its lightly spiced **boboties** and desserts. The cuisine's origins are Indonesian, though over the centuries other traditions have been influential: the curries and samoosas from India; puddings, tarts and biscuits from

the early Dutch settlers; sweet preserves from the French Huguenots. Also part of the South African experience is *potjiekos*, a long-simmering stew created with layers of meat, potatoes and a variety of vegetables in a large cast-iron pot, cooked over an open fire to allow the flavours to mingle.

Traditional African cooking does not appear on many South African menus. For most indigenous people, eating remains a practical and often formidably challenging necessity. The ordinary meal of the day in townships and villages is usually a simple affair of maize meal (samp), vegetables and, less often, stewed meat.

Something Special

Seafood (line-fish, crayfish and abalone) is usually excellent, though the shellfish tends to be rather expensive, especially in the urban centres where restaurant proprietors are accustomed to the pounds sterling and dollars of the ever-growing number of overseas visitors. Antelope **venison** (including springbok pie) is also something of a South African speciality, and ostrich steaks are becoming increasingly popular.

Above: *South Africa's pleasant climate lends itself to alfresco eating.*

Going Local
Biltong: strips of savoury dried meat.
Bobotie: light-textured curried meat topped with savoury custard.
Breyani: spicy Malay or Indian dish with rice and mutton or chicken.
Koeksister: deep-fried, plaited dough, soaked in syrup.
Konfyt: sweet preserve.
Naartjie: a citrus fruit similar to a mandarin or tangerine.
Sosatie: skewered meat and dried apricots marinated in a curry sauce, originating from the Indonesian 'satay'.
Snoek: a firm-fleshed, strongly flavoured fish, good for smoking and braaiing (*see* opposite).
Waterblommetjie bredie: a highly flavoured stew made with water lilies.

Right: *Freshly caught fish is on the menus of many coastal restaurants.*

The Cape's West Coast is famed for its seafood, freshly caught and often enjoyed in open-air restaurants that are noted for their wonderfully informal sociability.

Cape country fare, available in selected restaurants, evolved among rural Afrikaner communities, and is rich and filling, but the aromas and tastes are sublime indeed. Even tastier is **Malay cuisine** (*see* page 60). A firm favourite is *waterblommetjie bredie*, which is a stew made with indigenous water lilies.

A very select number of restaurants also offer something for exotic tastes: crocodile, snake, warthog and the like.

What to Drink

There are some 4000 South African **wines** on the market, ranging from full-bodied reds to delicate dry whites, all of which are drinkable and generally are very good. Some of the labels are fast gaining a reputation for excellence, a generous handful are quite sublime, and many are receiving accolades in international competitions. The wines are still fairly cheap by international standards, though prices have been rising. Some handy and informative volumes on the country's wines can be found in most bookshops. To discover the range of wines available embark on one or more of the Western Cape's **wine routes** (*see* pages 21).

A popular local drink that is becoming increasingly popular abroad is **rooibos tea**, a fragrant tea made from a herbal bush (*see* panel, page 66).

Where to Eat

South Africa's restaurants cater for all preferences and pockets; menus generally offer a wide range, from traditional fare and seafood, through Mediterranean, Cajun, Italian, Chinese, Indian and Mexican to French *haute cuisine*. Several eateries also double as taverns that occasionally feature live local music and entertainment. Some restaurants have outlets dotted throughout particular regions of the country, offering familiar fare all over. Some also have giant television sets for sports enthusiasts.

Bistros and coffee bars generally cater for the sophisticated crowd, while most of the fast-food outlets offer a good variety of 'food to go'.

Wines of the Cape
There are many experts who will send wine home or abroad for you:
Manuka Fine Wines
✉ Steenberg Village Shopping Centre, Tokai
☎ (021) 701-2046
💻 www.manuka.co.za
Vaughan Johnson's Wine Shop
✉ V & A Waterfront
☎ (021) 419-2121
📠 (021) 419-0040
The Vinyard Connection
✉ Stellenbosch
☎ (021) 884-4360
Oom Samie se Winkel,
✉ 84 Dorp Street, Stellenbosch
☎ (021) 887-2612
Steven Rom
✉ Sea Point
☎ (021) 439-6043
Wine-Of-The-Month-Club
✉ Claremont
☎ (021) 657-8100/81
📠 671-4992
Picardi Fine Wine and Spirits
✉ Foreshore, Cape Town
☎ (021) 425-1639/64

Left: *The famed Delaire wine estate.*

Gauteng and North-West

JOHANNESBURG

Gramadelas
Traditional Cape and African fare.
✉ *Market Theatre*,
☎ *(011) 838-6960.*

Kapitan's
Rather dingy but marvellous curries.
✉ *City centre*,
☎ *(011) 834-8048.*

Ile de France
Typically French provincial food
✉ *Cramerview*,
☎ *(011) 706-2837.*

Zoo Lake Restaurant
Continental cuisine in a pleasant setting.
✉ *Zoo Lake*,
☎ *(011) 646-8807.*

Linger Longer
Famed chef; French and Eastern fare.
✉ *Sandton*,
☎ *(011) 884-0465.*

Ferns Restaurant
African and cajun/creole buffet.
✉ *Sandton*,
☎ *(011) 780-5000.*

Osteria Tre Nanni
Best of Italian.
✉ *Parktown*,
☎ *(011) 327-0095.*

Gastriles
Superb food and award-winning wines.
✉ *Sandown*,
☎ *(011) 883-7399.*

Coco Bongo
Grills and African and continental cuisine.
✉ *Fourways*,
☎ *(011) 511-1826/7.*

Wine Gallery of Africa
International and African fusion in one of the city's top entertainment complexes.
✉ *MonteCasino, Fourways*,
☎ *(011) 511-1998.*

Milky Way Internet Café
Internet spot with light, good food.
✉ *Yeoville*,
☎ *(011) 487-3608.*

Gillooly's
Good food in splendid farmhouse setting.
✉ *Bedfordview*,
☎ *(011) 453-8066.*

PRETORIA

Lucit Candle Garden Theatre Restaurant
South African and African cuisine.
✉ *Rietondale*,
☎ *(012) 329-4180.*

Hillside Tavern
Splendid steaks in a relaxed atmosphere.
✉ *Lynnwood*,
☎ *(012) 348-1402.*

La Madelaine
Top award-winning French/Belgian bistro.
✉ *Lynnwood*,
☎ *(012) 361-3667.*

La Perla
Popular and well established, with seafood a speciality.
✉ *City centre*,
☎ *(012) 460-1267.*

Mostapha's
The chef here has worked for royalty!
✉ *Hatfield*,
☎ *(012) 362-0713.*

Gerard Moerdyk
Fine South African cuisine at its best.
✉ *Arcadia*,
☎ *(012) 344-4856.*

Limpopo and Mpumalanga

Guests at the lodges or private reserves are fully catered for, the cuisine excellent. Picnic lunches are often provided if prior notice is given. Generally, lodges will accept dinner guests not staying at the lodge, but reservations are essential. Larger resorts have restaurant facilities.

KwaZulu-Natal

DURBAN

Langoustine by the Sea

Seafood highlights, with excellent prawn curries and the like.
✉ *Durban North*,
☎ *(031) 563-7324,*

Razzmatazz

Porcupine kebabs and zebra pie for the adventurous diner.
✉ *City centre,*
☎ *(031) 561-5847.*

Ulundi

Great Indian food!
✉ *Royal Hotel,*
☎ *(031) 333-6000.*

Villa D'Este

Seafood and Italian of the highest quality.
✉ *City centre,*
☎ *(031) 202-7920.*

PIETERMARITZBURG

Da Vinci's

Wholesome Italian food that is both hearty and tasty.
✉ *Pietermaritzburg,*
☎ *(033) 345-5172.*

DRAKENSBERG

Royal Natal National Park

Traditional South African fare mixed with contemporary.
✉ *Mont-aux-Source,*
☎ *(036) 438-6303.*

Above: *An exotic lunch, served on banana leaves.*

Fast Food: Dining on the Blue Train

South Africa's Blue Train offers the ultimate in luxury travel. The 16-coach, 107-berth train leaves from Pretoria station, stopping at Johannesburg before heading for Cape Town. Passengers get to see spectacular scenery, especially from the elegantly appointed dining car where gourmet meals are served. Contact Satour,
☎ (011) 778-8000.

Below: *Farm stalls are situated along rural roads throughout the country.*

Eastern Cape

PORT ELIZABETH

Aviemore

Up-market, with local venison and seafoods.
⊠ *City centre,*
☎ *(041) 585-1125.*

De Kelder

Haute cuisine and a fine wine list.
⊠ *Summerstrand,*
☎ *(041) 583-2750.*

Café Brazilia

Finger-licking Portuguese fare.
⊠ *Humewood,*
☎ *(041) 585-1482.*

Natti's Thai Kitchen

Truly outstanding Thai food.
⊠ *Clyde,*
☎ *(041) 585-4301.*

GRAHAMSTOWN

La Galleria

Conventional Italian meals that are both tasty and well priced.
⊠ *New Street,*
☎ *(046) 622-2345.*

The Cock House

In-house restaurant of the acclaimed country hotel, specializing in stylish Provencal.
⊠ *Market Street,*
☎ *(046) 636-1295.*

EAST LONDON

Movenpick

Superb seafood fare.
⊠ *Orient Beach.*

Thatch Guest House

Excellent food, but by appointment only.
⊠ *Beacon Bay,*
☎ *(043) 748-6227.*

The Garden Route and Little Karoo

PLETTENBERG BAY

Stromboli's Inn

Fine country dining, with a hint of the sophisticated.
✉ Town centre,
☎ (044) 532-7710.

The Islander

A truly fabulous seafood buffet.
✉ 8km (4.5 miles) from town, towards Knysna,
☎ (044) 532-7776.

Bothers Restaurant and Terrace

Popular for breakfasts and lunches in an appealing décor.
✉ Main Street,
☎ (044) 533-5056.

Cornuti al Mare

Some splendid Italian wining and dining.
✉ Town centre,
☎ (044) 533-1277.

Tarn Country House

Truly spectacular surrounds, but dinner by appointment only.
✉ The Crags,
☎ (044) 534-8835.

KNYSNA

Oyster Tasting Tavern

Sample the finest seafood this resort town has to offer.
✉ Thesen's Island,
☎ (044) 382-6941.

Knysna Hollow Restaurant

Discerning menu that includes food that is very well prepared.
✉ on the country estate near town,
☎ (044) 382-5401.

Brenton Beach Restaurant

A fine á la carte menu and buffet, as well as remarkable views.
✉ Brenton Beach,
☎ (044) 381-0081.

MOSSEL BAY

The Gannet

Mainly seafood, but all rather good.
✉ Bartolomeu Dias Museum complex,
☎ (044) 691-1885.

Jazzbury's

Ethnic specialities, such as mopane worms.
✉ Town centre,
☎ (044) 691-1923.

Edward Charles: The Manor Hotel

Fine dining, but bookings essential.
✉ Sixth Avenue,
☎ (044) 690-7242.

GEORGE

The Copper Pot

A traditional Cape bistro menu in an old homestead setting.
✉ Town centre,
☎ (044) 870-7378.

Reel 'n Rustic

Plenty of good seafood, excellent grain-fed beef dishes, and decadent desserts.
✉ Town centre,
☎ (044) 884-0707.

OUDTSHOORN

Saddles Steak Ranch

Value-for-money steak, grills, pasta and pizza from a popular nationwide chain.
✉ Town centre,
☎ (044) 272-8054.

Jemima's

Eclectic menu, but mostly dishes of the region (ostrich!).
✉ Town centre,
☎ (044) 272-0808.

Western Cape

CAPE TOWN

Africa Café

Ethnic dishes from throughout Africa.

✉ 108 Shortmarket Street,

☎ (021) 422-0221.

Anatoli

Turkish fare in Middle Eastern surrounds.

✉ Napier Street,

☎ (021) 419-2501.

Bukhara

Excellent Indian cuisine; lunch and dinner.

✉ 33 Church Street,

☎ (021) 424-0000.

Floris Smit Huis

International focus.

✉ Corner Church and Loop Streets,

☎ (021) 423-3414/5,

The Grill Room

Elegant and old-style; continental cuisine.

✉ Mount Nelson,

☎ (021) 483-1000,

Maria's

Small Greek restaurant; excellent fare.

✉ 31 Barnet Street,

☎ (021) 461-8887.

Miller's Thumb

Locals' favourite, with excellent fish fare.

✉ 10b Kloofnek Road,

☎ (021) 424-3838.

Aubergine

Superb service, varied menu (mostly Cape and German dishes).

✉ 39 Barnet Street,

☎ (021) 465-4909,

Rozenhof

Classic menu with a variety of fine food.

✉ 18 Kloof Street,

☎ (021) 424-1968,

Mama Africa

African continental and lively bar popular with foreign visitors.

✉ 178 Long Street,

☎ (021) 424-8634,

Vasco da Gama Taverna

A friendly Portuguese restaurant, attractively downmarket.

✉ 3 Alfred Street,

☎ (021) 425-2157.

Savoy Cabbage

Eclectic cuisine, very trendy place.

✉ 101 Hout Street,

☎ (021) 424-2626,

WATERFRONT

Alabama

Wine and dine while cruising the harbour.

✉ 6 Quay 5,

☎ (082) 672-9621.

Ferryman's Tavern

Converted railway shed with good beer.

✉ East Pier Road,

☎ (021) 419-7748.

The Green Dolphin

Seafood, pasta. Good jazz played nightly.

✉ Alfred Mall,

☎ (021) 421-7471/5.

Morton's on the Wharf

Tasty New Orleans-style Cajun food.

✉ Victoria Wharf,

☎ (021) 418-3633.

Quay 4

Lively outdoor tavern with a smarter restaurant venue upstairs.

☎ (021) 419-2008,

✆ (021) 421-2056.

Bayfront Blu

Seafood and African dishes, superb views.

✉ Two Oceans Aquarium, Dock Road,

☎ (021) 419-9068.

Atlantic Seaboard

Blues
Fine Californian and Mediterranean food.
✉ Camps Bay,
☎ (021) 438-2040/1.

Europa
Elegant old house, serving seafood.
✉ Sea Point,
☎ (021) 439-2820.

Peninsula

Buitenverwachting
Very formal, Deluxe award winner.
✉ Constantia,
☎ (021) 794-3522.

Peddlars
Country fare in rural surrounds; popular.
✉ Constantia,
☎ (021) 794-7747.

Constantia Uitsig
Fine Mediterranean Provençal cuisine.
✉ Constantia,
☎ (021) 794-4480.

The Brass Bell
Popular with locals; overlooks the harbour, excellent seafood.
✉ Kalk Bay,
☎ (021) 788-5456/55.

Winelands

De Akker
Good hearty pub food.
✉ Stellenbosch,
☎ (021) 883-3512.

Lanzerac
Formal and very good.
✉ Stellenbosch,
☎ (021) 887-1132.

D'Ouwe Werf
Excellent Cape dishes.
✉ Stellenbosch,
☎ (021) 887-4608/.

Lord Neethling
Cape and Continental.
✉ Stellenbosch,
☎ (021) 883-8966.

De Volkskombuis
Traditional Cape.
✉ Stellenbosch,
☎ (021) 887-2121.

La Maison de Chamonix
Cosy for whole family.
✉ Franschhoek,
☎ (021) 876-2393.

La Petite Ferme
French and local food.
✉ Franschhoek,
☎ (021) 876-3016/8.

Le Ballon Rouge
French-SA fusion.
✉ Franschhoek,
☎ (021) 876-2651.

Le Quartier Français
View from every table.
✉ Franschhoek,
☎ (021) 876-2151.

Boschendal
Le Pique-Nique!
✉ Franschhoek,
☎ (021) 870-4274.

Bosman's
Fine gourmet cuisine.
✉ Paarl,
☎ (021) 863-2727.

Rhebokskloof
Acclaimed wine estate.
✉ Paarl,
☎ (021) 869-8606.

Garden Terrace
Cape Malay carvery.
✉ Somerset West,
☎ (021) 855-1040.

L'Auberge du Paysan
Top French dining.
✉ Somerset West,
☎ (021) 842-2008.

96 Winery Road
Provençal and eastern.
✉ Zandberg Farm, Winery Road,
☎ (021) 842-2020.

Gold Reef City Casino
✉ Johannesburg
☎ (011) 248-5000

Sun City Casino
✉ Pilanesberg (N4 Freeway to Rustenburg)
☎ (014) 557-1000

Carousel Entertainment World
✉ N1 Freeway to Pietersburg
☎ (012) 718-7477

Morula Sun
✉ Mabopane Freeway, Route R80
☎ (012) 799-0000

GrandWest Casino
✉ Goodwood
☎ (021) 505-7777

Club Mykonos Casino
✉ Cape West Coast
☎ (022) 707-6000

Caledon Spa Casino
✉ Caledon
☎ (028) 214-1271

ENTERTAINMENT
Casinos

Following decades of strict restrictions on gambling, South Africa's gaming laws eased off considerably with the emergence of democracy. Horse-racing was always legal because it was said to be based on skill rather than chance, but there are now some 40 casinos in operation or development.

The most popular of these casino-cum-entertainment complexes include **Gold Reef City** in Johannesburg (*see* page 14) and the all-time favourite **Sun City** (*see* page 16) in the Pilanesberg. Pretoria, on the other hand, boasts the **Carousel Entertainment World** and the **Morula Sun**.

The Cape selection ranges from the glitzy **GrandWest** just north of Cape Town, which offers entertainment for both adults and children; the **Club Mykonos** resort on the West Coast; and the Overberg's **Caledon Spa**.

All of these relatively new complexes offer roulette, blackjack and poker, as well as slot machines and other table games.

Theatres

South Africa's arts calendar is a lively one indeed, and one that showcases not only indigenous theatre and music, but also a wide spectrum of international-standard productions. The most spectacular performances – drama, opera,

ballet, oratorio and occasionally lavish musical – are usually staged at established theatre and show venues.

The **Market Theatre Complex** in Johannesburg's Newtown Cultural Precinct specializes in live experimental theatre that draws on the African experience.

The **Civic Theatre** in Braamfontein is a 1120-seat venue for drama, opera, ballet, light musical productions, concerts, recitals and other shows, while symphonic music can be heard at the **Linder Auditorium** at the Johannesburg College of Education.

Pretoria's **State Theatre** has five venues, and apart from its regular shows, stages concerts on Sunday afternoons.

Durban's **Playhouse** has seven theatres, the décor a mix of Tudor and Moorish, reflecting its past as a great 'picture palace'.

Artscape (The Nico) on Cape Town's Foreshore boasts three auditoriums which stage many international shows. Many smaller local productions feature at **The Baxter**, which has a 600-plus capacity. There's also a small studio/workshop.

Comic fare in the Mother City is generally staged in Camps Bay's revamped **Theatre on the Bay**. There are also a number of smaller, intimate theatres: check the local press for up-to-date details on the theatre scene.

Above: *A traditional Zulu performance at the Market Theatre.*
Opposite: *GrandWest Casino is the Cape's most impressive.*

Market Theatre
✉ Newtown
☎ (011) 832-1641

Civic Theatre
✉ Braamfontein
☎ (011) 877-6800

Linder Auditorium
✉ Johannesburg
☎ (011) 717-3007

State Theatre
✉ Pretoria
☎ (012) 322-1665

The Playhouse
✉ Durban
☎ (031) 369-9555

Artscape
✉ Cape Town CBD
☎ (021) 410-9800

The Baxter
✉ Rondebosch
☎ (021) 685-7880

Theatre on the Bay
✉ Camps Bay
☎ (021) 438-3301

Above: *Minstrels take to Cape Town's streets at New Year.*

Cape Town City Hall
✉ Cape Town CBD
☎ (021) 400-2230

V & A Amphitheatre
✉ V & A Waterfront
☎ (021) 408-7600

Kirstenbosch
✉ Newlands
☎ (021) 799-8899

Oude Libertas Centre
✉ Stellenbosch
☎ (021) 809-7000

The IMAX Experience
The V & A Waterfront's BMW Pavilion is home to the the giant IMAX cinema – the world's largest film format, projected onto a five-storey screen, and with powerful digital sound.
✉ Portswood Road
☎ (021) 419-7365
✆ (021) 419-7791
🖥 www.imax.co.za
✆ imax@numetro.co.za

Music

As in the rest of Africa, music plays a vital role in South African society, and has many different faces and sounds.

For people's music, try the Sakayi nightclub in Rosebank, Johannesburg, and the Mozambique club in Hillbrow, while jazz is at its best at the legendary Kippie's Jazz Bar in Newtown.

Evening concerts are performed in Cape Town's **City Hall**, while other venues include the Waterfront's open-air **Ampitheatre** and the **Kirstenbosch** gardens.

On the fringes of Stellenbosch is the **Oude Libertas Centre**, best known for its Sunday concerts in the 430-seat amphitheatre. Held December to March, concerts range from jazz to traditional African sounds. **Spier's** open-air amphitheatre also offers jazz, classical and light music in summer.

Generally, African people have a natural gift for rhythm, harmony and spontaneous song. Zulu instruments are few and simple – a double-ended cowhide drum, a rattle worn on the ankle or shaken by hand, a reed pipe. But there is also the powerful roar of men's voices in part harmony, the descant of the women, the clapping of hands and the stamping of feet. Other groups create music using xylophones, marimbas and stringed instruments.

Generally, plenty of live music – jazz, pop, cabaret – feature on South Africa's night scene. Venues and performers change all the time; for the latest information, consult local tourism offices or entertainment and leisure guides available from major bookshops.

Outdoor Entertainment

Much of the social life of South Africans takes place in the great outdoors, which it has in great abundance, from the bushveld and its reserves to rugged mountain landscapes and endless beaches.

Even big cities have outdoor diversions. In Johannesburg, visit the **Florence Bloom Bird Sanctuary** in Delta Park, **Jo'burg Zoo** in Parkview, Emmarentia's **Botanical Gardens**, **Lion Park** north of the city, the **Lipizzaners** at Kyalami, **Melrose Bird Sanctuary** and the **Midrand Snake Park**.

Pretoria, on the other hand, boasts the **National Botanical Garden**, the **Moreleta Spruit** trail in Lynnwood Glen, and **Wonderboom Nature Reserve** on Voortrekker Road.

Of course, coastal regions have their own special draw cards, notably the beaches. Swimmers and surfers flock to Durban's **Golden Mile** in summer. The shore from **Blue Lagoon** to **Addington** (and others on to the north and south) is protected by shark nets and patrolled by lifeguards. **Bay of Plenty** hosts the international surf competition.

Port Elizabeth is ideal for nature rambles: **St George's Park**, **Settlers Park**, **Baakens River Gorge**, the **Island Conservation Area** near Sea View, and **Van Stadens Flower Reserve** all offer delightfully green retreats.

While Cape Town is most famous for the exquisite beaches of its Atlantic Seaboard, especially at **Clifton**, **Camps Bay**, **Llandudno** and **Sandy Bay**, the white beaches at **Hout Bay**, **Noordhoek**, **Muizenberg**, **Boulders** and **Fish Hoek** are splendid (and warmer!). Of course, there are also long stretches of sand beyond the Peninsula at **Langebaan** and **Blouberg**, **Gordon's Bay** and **The Strand**.

Tips for Hikers
• Don't underestimate mountains and the dangers they conceal. Storms and bad weather can descend in minutes. Take warm clothing however balmy the day; don't wear new boots; pack more food than you think you'll need.
• Do your homework: map-reading and route-charting are vital. Notify friends, family or reserve officials of your route and the time you expect to be back.
• Maps of paths and trails are, for the most part, readily available from book shops .
• Don't venture up on your own: a hiking party ideally comprises three people. Your first outings should be with an experienced hiker/climber.

Below: *The Oude Libertas amphitheatre in Stellenbosch is renowned for its concerts.*

Right: *A hot air balloon safari provides a unique view of the Magaliesberg.*

Tour Operators
GAUTENG AND NORTH-WEST
Ambula Art Safaris
Local arts and crafts.
☎ *(011) 794-2770.*

Bill Harrop's Original Balloon Safaris
Gauteng from the air.
☎ *(011) 705-3201.*

Chamber of Mines
Tours underground.
☎ *(011) 498-7100.*

Dumela Africa
Say hello to Africa!
☎ *(083) 659-9928.*

Egoli Tours
See the City of Gold.
☎ *(011) 888-8927.*

Gold Reef Guides
Tours of the Reef.
☎ *(011) 496-1400.*

Jimmy's Face to Face Tours
Visit the townships.
☎ *(011) 331-6109.*

Luxliner Tours
Sightsee in comfort.
☎ *(011) 914-3222.*

Ma-Africa Tours
Good, friendly guides.
☎ *(011) 984-2561.*

Parktown Tours
Discover local heritage.
☎ *(011) 482-3349.*

Springbok Atlas
Take a tour in comfort.
☎ *(011) 396-1053.*

Gauteng Tourism
✉ Rosebank Mall, Rosebank
☎ (011) 327-2000

Tourism Johannesburg
✉ Village Walk, Sandton
☎ (011) 784-1352

Pretoria Tourist Information Centre
✉ Church Square, Pretoria
☎ (012) 337-4487

South African National Parks
(central reservations)
☎ (012) 428-9111
🖳 www.parks-sa.co.za
🖰 reservations@parks-sa.co.za

Welcome Tours & Safaris
Witness the unusual.
☎ *(082) 415-4325.*

Indula Safaris
See the real Pretoria.
☎ *(012) 811-0197.*

Sakabula Safaris
Explore the capital.
☎ *(083) 460-3097.*

Zambezi Spectacular
Wild water adventure.
☎ *(011) 794-1707.*

Imbizo Tours
Township tours.
☎ *(011) 838-2667.*

Student Travel Association
Budget options for all.
☎ *(011) 447-5414.*

Mpumalanga and Limpopo
Hamba Kahle Tours
Escarpment wonders.
☎ *(013) 741-1618.*

Safari Siligato
Lowveld exploration.
☎ *(013) 752-6093.*

Sight, Sound & Smell
African adventure.
☎ *(013) 744-7063.*

Solitaire Tours
Fine safari experience.
☎ *(013) 752-4527.*

Vula Tours
Discover the Lowveld.
☎ *(013) 752-6093.*

Lowveld Tours
Escarpment environs.
☎ *(013) 755-1988.*

Kruger National Park
☎ (013) 735-4030

Mpumalanga Tourism Authority
✉ Nelspruit
☎/✆ (013) 752-7001

Lowveld Tourism Johannesburg
✉ Shop 5 (Satour Information), Promenade Centre, Nelspruit
☎ (013) 755-1988

Sondela Tourist Information
✉ Old Trading Post, Main Street, Sabie
☎ (013) 764-3492

Below: *Most tour operators in the Pilanesberg include stops at The Lost City.*

Durban Unlimited
✉ Tourist Junction,
Old Station Building,
Pine Street, Durban
☎ (031) 304-4934
📠 (031) 304-3868

**Tourism
KwaZulu-Natal**
✉ (see above)
☎ (031) 304-7144
📠 (031) 304-8792
🖥 www.
tourism-kzn.org

**Drakensberg Tourism
Association**
✉ Hotel Walter,
Bergville
☎ (036) 448-1557

**KwaZulu-Natal
Nature Conservation**
(Pietermaritzburg)
☎ (033) 845-1002
☎ (031) 201-3126

**Garden Route
Central Reservations**
☎ (044) 874-7474 /
873-3222

Garden Route Tourism
☎ (044) 873-6314/55
📠 (044) 884-0688

Knysna Tourism
☎ (044) 382-6960

**Mossel Bay
Tourism Bureau**
☎ (044) 691-2202

Plettenberg Bay Info
☎ (044) 533-4065

KWAZULU-NATAL

Durban Unlimited
Historical walkabouts.
☎ *(031) 304-4934.*

Exec-U-Tours
Overland and city
tours.
☎ *(031) 563-0087.*

Strelitzia Tours
Visitor's favourite.
☎ *(031) 266-9480.*

Blue Dolphin
Tourist Service
Exciting adventure
sports.
☎ *(031) 207-5138.*

African Horseback
Safaris
Horse riding and
more.
☎ *(031) 561-4780.*

Umhlanga Tours
Explore the coast.
☎ *(031) 561-3777.*

Helicopters
Unlimited
Bird's-eye views.
☎ *(031) 564-0176.*

Tekweni Eco Tours
Venture beyond the
city.
☎ *(031) 303-1199.*

EASTERN CAPE

Sunshine Service
A 24-hour tour service.
☎ *(042) 293-1911.*

Calabash Tours
'Real City Tours'.
☎ *(041) 585-6162.*

Fundani Tours
Battlefield routes.
☎ *(041) 454-2064.*

Tanaqua Tours
Hikes and history.
☎ *(083) 270-9924.*

Pembury Tours
Big-game adventures.
☎ *(041) 581-2581.*

GARDEN ROUTE

Ecobound Tours
& Travel
Ecotourism at its best.
☎ *(044) 871-4455.*

Horseback Trails
Hike in the Zuurberg.
☎ *(042) 233-0583.*

Southern Cape
Herbarium
Flower Route.
☎ *(044) 874-1558.*

MTN Whale Route
Spot the whales!
☎ *(044) 873-4343.*

WESTERN CAPE

Wineland Ballooning

Champagne in the air.

☎ *(021) 863-3192.*

Felix Unite River Adventures

Canoeing and more.

☎ *(021) 670-1300.*

River Rafters

Ride the Cape waters.

☎ *(021) 712-5094.*

Hylton Ross

Package coach tours.

☎ *(021) 511-1784.*

Mother City Tours

The best of the Cape.

☎ *(021) 488-3817.*

Game Fishing Safaris

Fish southern waters.

☎ *(021) 674-2203.*

Civair

Hover over the Cape.

☎ *(021) 419-5182.*

Court Helicopters

Go for a whirl!

☎ *(021) 934-3693.*

Spier Wine Estate

Wineland fun.

☎ *(021) 809-1100.*

Face Adrenalin

Hold your breath!

☎ *(021) 712-5839.*

Coastal Kayak

Take to the waters.

☎ *(021) 439-1134.*

One City Tours

Beyond the city limits.

☎ *(021) 387-5351.*

Grassroutes Tours

Something different.

☎ *(021) 424-8480.*

Cape Town Tourism Visitor's Centre
✉ Burg Street, Cape Town
☎ (021) 426-4260

V & A Waterfront Visitor's Centre
☎ (021) 408-7600

Winelands Regional Tourism
☎ (021) 872-0686
📞 (021) 872-0534

Stellenbosch Publicity Association
☎ (021) 883-3584 / 883-9633
📞 (021) 883-8071

Below: *Cape Town's topless bus provides scenic tours of the city.*

Hermanus
Location: Map F–C3
Distance from Cape Town: 140km
(85 miles)

Betty's Bay/ Pringle Bay
Location: Map F–B3
Distance from Cape Town: 110km
(68 miles)

Kleinmond
Location: Map F–C3
Distance from Cape Town: 120km
(75 miles)

False Bay
Location: Map F–B3
Distance from CBD: 24km (15 miles)

Lambert's Bay
Location: Map E–C5
Distance from Cape Town: 320km
(200 miles)

Below: *Hermanus remains the most favoured spot on the Cape coast for whale-watching.*

EXCURSIONS

Beyond the bleak Cape Flats, to the north and east of Cape Town, the land rises to the splendid upland ranges of the coastal rampart. The mountains – part of what is known as the Cape fold mountains – are high, their lower slopes and the valleys in between are green and fertile, mantled by pastures and orchards and, especially, by vineyards heavy with fruit.

Whale-watching

Whale-watching off the Cape coast is one of South Africa's fastest-growing tourist pastimes, and it is the town of **Hermanus**, nestled on the edge of **Walker Bay**, that serves as the whale-watching 'capital'. In the autumn and winter months these giant marine mammals, most being southern rights, come inshore, occasionally with a calf in tow. An official 'whale crier', complete with uniform and horn, announces the arrival of these leviathans.

But Hermanus is not the only stop on the unofficial 'whale-watching route', and a number of secluded bays on the southern and western Cape coast offer plenty of opportunity to spot whales, as well as dolphins occasionally. The most popular of these are Betty's Bay, Kleinmond, Onrus, False Bay and even the fishing settlements along the Cape West Coast and as far afield as Lambert's Bay.

The Escarpment

The Escarpment is a land of diversity, a spectacular mixture of forested massifs and high buttresses, sculpted peaks and deep ravines, crystal streams and delicate waterfalls, and of

green valleys along which flow the **Olifants** and **Crocodile** rivers and their multiple tributaries. The uplands are not as dramatic as their counterparts to the south, the KwaZulu-Natal's **Drakensberg** (*see* page 18); on the other hand, they're a lot more accessible to the ordinary traveller: the roads are in good condition, the hotels and hideaways plentiful and inviting.

Lydenburg, fly-fishing haven of Mpumalanga, is a rather attractive and thriving town; the town museum, trout hatchery and nature reserve nearby are well worth visiting. Higher up the hills is **Sabie**, once a gold town and now centre of the forestry industry (the museum has some fascinating exhibits). Situated on the scenic Kowyn's Pass road (itself a spectacular throughway to the Lowveld below), is the pretty **Graskop** village. Lisbon Falls, near Graskop, is one of the Escarpment's myriad beautiful cascades. To the southwest is **Dullstroom**, whose railway station is the highest in southern Africa. Dullstroom has two enchanting hotels and a number of nearby luxury lodges, many of which cater for the fishing and angling enthusiasts. The area is particularly well known for its trout streams and dams.

Above: *Green valleys surround Mpumalanga's Crocodile River.*

Waterfall Route
The unofficial Waterfall Route takes in eight waterfalls in the Sabie-Graskop vicinity. The most attractive are:
Bridal Veil (aptly named)
MacMac with twin cataracts, drops into dense ravine, then runs into the MacMac Pools
Lone Creek, 68m (222ft); mist-forest
Horseshoe, a beautiful national monument
Berlin plunges 48m (158ft) into a pool
Lisbon, a beautiful twin waterfall

Both the Berlin and the Lisbon falls have observation points and picnic sites.

Below: *Young Zulu girls, or* intombi, *in rural areas may still wear traditional dress on occasion.*

Shakaland

The term 'Zululand' refers to the area stretching north from the **Thukela (Tugela) River**, the traditional seat of Zulu power and once home to the legendary **King Shaka**.

The British settlement of Port Natal (Durban) in the 1820s coincided with the **Mfecane**, which was triggered by the rise of Shaka. His newly fashioned army had set out in conquest, igniting a chain reaction of violence and counterviolence that engulfed the entire east coast. When Shaka finally succeeded to the Zulu chieftainship in 1816, the Zulu numbered just 1500 people – but within a few years the 'warrior king' controlled the entire eastern (KwaZulu-Natal) seaboard. The keys to this phenomenal expansion were the new weapons and fighting techniques Shaka introduced to his fighting regimen (*see* panel, page 8).

Today, a cultural route offers authentic kraals and tangible reminders of historical battles. Inland, the picturesque **Nkwaleni Valley** is the location of **Shakaland**. One and a half hours from Durban, it comprises a hotel in the form of a village of beehive huts. Its drawcards include culinary specialities, traditional dance, displays by sangomas and herbalists, basket weaving, pot-making as well as hut-building. Contact Shakaland, ☎ (035) 460-0912.

The Great Fish River

Vast stretches of the Eastern Cape remain some of South Africa's most untouched wilderness. To the south of **East London** (the country's major river port), the coastline stretches for roughly 65km (40 miles) to the Great Fish River, north of **Port Alfred** (a picturesque resort with a marina and small

craft harbour). The estuary of the Great Fish is distinguished by its maze of caves, tunnels and blowholes, and by its birdlife.

Inland drawcards include two notable reserves, of contrasting character and vegetation. Largest and handiest to the coast is the **Great Fish River Wetland Reserve** (comprising Double Drift, Andries Vosloo and Sam Knott reserves), home to hippo, black rhino, buffalo and many antelope species, as well as San rock paintings. The reserve is open to day visitors, but, for those who wish to stay over, comfortable accommodation at a restored Victorian homestead and a private camp is available. **Tsolwana Game Reserve**, a magnificent mountain reserve, incorporates a tribal resource area which earns valuable tourism revenue for the community. Tsolwana hosts a variety of indigenous – rhino, giraffe, wildebeest and springbok – and exotic species, including the Himalayan tahr and fallow deer. The exotics are mainly kept for hunting. Self-catering accommodation is available in farmhouse lodges. Both reserves offer walking trails (with trained game guards), wildlife viewing roads, and hunting.

Above: *Port Alfred's delightful marina and small craft harbour.*

Wild Experiences
Shamwari Game Reserve is a private game sanctuary on the Bushman's River and home to a variety of animals, including the Big Five, in a malaria-free environment. Luxury accommodation is available in a converted Edwardian farmhouse, lodge and two houses. Much closer to the Great Fish River is **Tsolwana Game Reserve**. This enterprise provides funds for the local Xhosa community by offering game drives, hiking trails and, in the evening, tribal dancing.

Above: *Robben Island is separated from the mainland by 12km (7 miles) of open ocean.*

Off to the Island

Only the Robben Island Museum conducts official tours of the island. Bookings may be made through the Robben Island Information and Exhibition Centre;
☎ (021) 419-1300
✆ (021) 419-1057
✉ info@
robben-island.org.za
🕑 07:30–18:00, daily

Tickets may be bought at the Robben Island Museum and the embarkation point at Jetty 1, from where the Makana departs. The trip takes about an hour; tours may take up to three hours.

Robben Island

Just off the shore of **Table Bay**, to the west of the suburb of Milnerton and visible from the summit of Table Mountain, lies Robben Island, where **Nelson Mandela** was incarcerated as a political prisoner for much of his 27-year imprisonment.

Over the centuries, the island has served as a sheep farm, a penal settlement, a leper colony, a pauper camp, an infirmary and a lunatic asylum. It was recently proclaimed a **World Heritage Site**. Trips (arranged only through the official body, **Robben Island Museum**) take in the tiny cells (including Mandela's) and a drive across the sparsely vegetated 574ha (1418-acre) island to see **Robert Sobukwe's** prison home, as well as other historical buildings, including the **Church of the Good Shepherd** and the **Old Residency**. Visitors are ferried to the island in relative luxury, and the guides are generally ex-prisoners who spent time on the island during the apartheid years.

Tickets may be booked at the **Nelson Mandela Gateway** to Robben Island or the **Cape Town Visitor's Centre**.

The Four Passes Fruit Route

If you're in a motoring mood, the scenic **Four Passes** drive leads you from Cape Town to the Winelands town of Stellenbosch, and over **Helshoogte Pass**, which towers above the Drakenstein valley area. It then takes you past the Boschendal Estate and Franschhoek, over the rugged **Franschhoek Pass** and through the apple orchards of Elgin and Grabouw, before bringing you home over the Hottentots-Holland range via **Sir Lowry's Pass** and through Somerset West. You may also like to take **Viljoen's Pass** to Vyeboom and Villiersdorp.

If you feel inclined to taste a few wines, pay a visit to Anglo-American's new multi-million-rand wine cellar on the **Vergelegen Estate**. Designed by a Parisian architect, the winery is built into the hillside and offers a 360-degree view unequalled by any Cape wine farm. You can enjoy a light lunch or simply stay for tea; visits to the winery are by appointment only.

Nature lovers should not miss a visit to the nearby **Helderberg Nature Reserve**, which offers lovely scenery, as well as interesting flora and birdlife.

Food in Franschhoek
Le Quartier Français, Huguenot Road: award-winner, exquisite French-influenced, Cape-style cuisine, ☎ (021) 876-2151.
La Petite Ferme, Pass Road: sweeping views of the valley, great food, ☎ (021) 876-3016.
La Maison de Chamonix, Uitkyk Road: voted among the country's top three popular restaurants, ☎ (021) 876-2393.
Haute Cabriere, Pass Road: dine in the estate wine cellar, ☎ (021) 876-3688.
Polfyntjies, fresh country cooking, ☎ (021) 876-3217.

Left: *The scenic Helderberg Nature Reserve is rich in flora and fauna.*

Above: *Cape Town panorama, with Table Mountain rising above the city.*

Best Times to Visit

More visitors are travelling to the country all year round, but the best time for **Gauteng** and environs is the warm spring (Sep–Oct). **Lowveld** summers are hot and humid, and winters (Jun/Jul) sunny. The **Escarpment** has a kind climate all year, but best is Oct–Jan, before the rains. Winter (Jun–Aug) in **KwaZulu-Natal** is best as summer humidity can cause discomfort. Much of the **Eastern Cape** and **Western Cape** is fine Sep–Oct (spring), but at its balmy best in summer.

Tourist Information

Satour (South African Tourism Board) has offices in, among other places, the UK (London), USA (New York and LA), France (Paris), Germany (Frankfurt), Israel (Tel Aviv), Italy (Milan), Japan (Tokyo), Netherlands, Belgium and Scandinavia (main office Amsterdam), Switzerland (main office Zürich), Taiwan (Taipei), and Zimbabwe (Harare). Satour's headquarters: ⊠ 12 Rivonia Road, Illovo, ☎ (011) 778-8000. It operates regional offices in main centres. The country is well represented on the Internet; quickest and most efficient way to find out more about South African destinations and other tourist information is via the **Ananzi South Africa** search engine: 🖳 www.ananzi.co.za Main centres and tourist areas also have **publicity associations** that provide up-to-date information, free of charge, on everything from recreation to transport and accommodation. Contact addresses and telephone numbers for many of these appear in the relevant chapters of this book. **Computicket**, which has branches countrywide, handles most concert, theatre and cinema bookings. For contact details, consult the relevant telephone directory for a specific region.

Entry Requirements

All visitors need a valid passport for entry into South Africa. Most foreign nationals, however, are exempt from visa requirements, including citizens of the United States, Canada and the European Community, as well as the following countries: Australia, Austria, Botswana, Brazil, Chile, Ireland, Japan, Namibia, New Zealand, Singapore and Switzerland.

Health Requirements

Visitors from or passing through a yellow fever zone (most of tropical Africa and South America) must produce an International Certificate of Vaccination. Air travellers who only pass through the airports of such a zone are exempt. Note that cholera and smallpox certificates are not needed, and no AIDS screening is in force.

Getting There

By air: Major points of entry are Johannesburg and Cape Town's international airports. Durban's also has international status. South African Airways serves Bloemfontein, Cape Town, Durban, East London, George, Johannesburg, Kimberley, Port Elizabeth, Pretoria, Nelspruit, Pietersburg/Polokwane, Mmabatho, Upington. Small airlines serves lesser towns and main tourist stops. Charter services are available.

By road: South Africa has an extensive and well-signposted road network comprising some 200,000km (124,280 miles) of highways. Surfaces are generally in good condition, though the going can be rugged in country areas.

Transport

Driver's licence: You must carry this with you at all times. Zimbabwe, Mozambique, Namibia, Botswana, Lesotho and Swaziland licences are valid in South Africa. So too are other foreign licences, provided they carry a photograph and are either printed in English or accompanied by an English-language certificate of authenticity. Alternatively, obtain an International Driving Permit before your departure.

Road rules and signs: In South Africa, one drives on the left. The general speed limit on national highways, urban freeways and other major routes is 120kph (75mph); on secondary (rural) roads 100kph (60mph), and in built-up areas 60kph (35mph) unless otherwise indicated. The main roads are identified by colour and number rather than by name. Using a good map (one that incorporates the route marker system), the visitor should have little trouble finding his/her way around city and country.

Car hire: Avis, Imperial (incorporating Hertz), Budget and other, smaller, rental firms are well represented in the major centres. Airports and some of the bigger game parks have car-hire facilities.

Insurance: Your vehicle must be covered by a Third Party Insurance policy; car-rental firms will make appropriate arrangements; for overland visitors, insurance tokens are available at Beitbridge and other major border control posts.

Maps: Some excellent regional and city maps are available from Satour, the Auto-mobile Association, from major book stores and airport kiosks. Recommended are those in the *Globetrotter* series.

Petrol: Cities, towns and main routes are generally very well served by filling stations. Many of these stay open 24 hours a day, others ⏲ 06:00–18:00. Petrol, either Super or Premium, is sold in litres. Note that on the Highveld, because of its altitude, the petrol has a lower octane rating (Super is 93, Premium 87; while on the coast, Super is 97 and Premium 93). Rather use the Super or Premium rating as a guide. Pump attend-ants see to your fuel and other needs.

The Automobile Association: The AA is the country's biggest motoring club, and provides a wide range of services, including assistance with break-downs and other emergencies, accommodation reservations and advice on touring, caravanning, camping, places of interest, insurance and car hire. Maps and brochures are available. These services are offered to visitors who belong to the AA or affiliated motoring organization.

AA headquarters:
⊠ AA House, 66 Korte Street, Braamfontein (Johannesburg) 2001, ☎ (011) 799-1000. For the AA offices in the other centres, consult the relevant telephone directory.

Coach travel: Luxury coach services link the major centres (Greyhound, Intercape Ferreira, Translux, Trancity), and tour operators spread the network wider, taking in the country's game parks and reserves, scenic attractions and other tourist venues. For details, consult your travel agent or the local publicity association.

What to Pack

South Africa enjoys long hot summers and generally mild winters; folk dress informally, though 'smart casual' is often required after dark at theatres and other entertainment venues, and at the more sophisticated hotels and restaurants. Beach wear is acceptable only on the beach; casual clothing is customary at resorts and in the game areas.

For summer (Oct–Apr), pack lightweight garments and a hat but include a jacket or jersey for cooler, and occasionally chilly, nights. Most of the country has summer rainfall, so bring an umbrella or raincoat. For winter, be sure to pack warm clothing.

Money Matters

The South African currency unit is the Rand, divided into 100 cents. Coins are issued in denominations of 1c, 5c, 10c, 20c, 50c, R1, R2 and R5; notes

in denominations of R5, R10, R20, R50, R100 and R200. Coinage designs have changed, and some denominations circulate in two forms; beware the superficial similarity between smaller and larger denominations. Most supermarkets and convenience stores round off the cost of purchases to 5c.

Currency exchange: Currency can be converted into rands at banks, Bureaux de Change and through authorized dealers such as Thomas Cook and American Express.

Banks: Banking hours in major centres ⊕ 09:00–15:30 on weekdays and 08:30/ 09:00–11:00 Sat. There are currency exchange and banking facilities at the international airports. Traveller's cheques can be cashed at banking institutions and at many hotels and shops.

Credit cards: Most hotels, restaurants, companies, shops, and

Public Holidays

1 January • New Year's Day
March/April • Good Friday, Family Day, Easter Monday
21 March • Human Rights Day
27 April • Freedom Day
1 May • Workers' Day
16 June • Youth Day
9 August • National Women's Day
24 September • Heritage Day
16 December • Day of Reconciliation
25 December • Christmas Day
26 December • Day of Goodwill

tour operators accept international credit cards (American Express, Diners' Club, Bank of America, Visa, MasterCard). But you cannot buy petrol with a credit card.

Value Added Tax: VAT, currently at 14 per cent, is levied on most goods (basic foods are exempt). Foreign visitors can claim back tax paid on goods to be taken out of the country and whose total value exceeds R250. For this you need to present (at point of exit) your passport, the goods and relevant invoices.

Tipping: Provided the service is satisfactory, it's usual to tip porters, waiters/waitresses, taxi drivers, room attendants, golf caddies and car guards. Tipping petrol attendants is optional, though a window-wash and a smile merit recognition. Gratuities for quantifiable services (waiters, taxi drivers) should amount to at least

10 per cent of the cost of the service; for nonquantifiable services of a minor nature (porterage, for example) it's customary to offer a tip of plus-minus R5.

Service charges: Hotels may not by law levy a charge for general services (though there's often a telephone service loading, sometimes a hefty one). While restaurants are indeed entitled to levy such a charge, few do.

Business Hours

Normal trading and business hours are ☉ 08:30–17:00 Mon–Fri, 08:30–13:00 Sat. Most supermarkets stay open till 18:00, later on Fridays, and on Saturday afternoons and Sunday mornings. Corner cafés and suburban mini-markets stay open from early to late every day of the week. Liquor stores close at 18:30. Most of the major shopping malls offer night shopping.

Time Difference

Throughout the year, South African Standard Time is two hours ahead of Greenwich Mean (or Universal Standard) Time, one hour ahead of European Winter Time, and seven hours ahead of United States Eastern Standard Winter Time.

Communications

The telephone system is fully automatic; and one can dial direct to most parts of the world. The telephone directory lists dialling codes. Both local and long-distance calls are metred. Dial 1023 for directory queries. Fax facilities are widely available. Public call boxes accept coins or Telkom phone cards. Most post offices are ⏰ 08:00–16:30 weekdays and 08:00–12:00 Sat. An international priority mail service is available. Stamps are usually available at some stationers and cafès and super-markets.

Embassies and Consulates

Most countries have diplomatic representation in South Africa, maintaining their principal offices in Pretoria. They are listed in the Yellow Pages (under Consulates and Embassies) and in telephone directories (listed under the country's name).

Electricity

Generally, urban power systems are 220/230 volts AC at 50 cycles a second; Pretoria's system generates 250 volts; Port Elizabeth's 220/250 volts. Plugs are 5-amp 2-pin or 15-amp 3-pin (round pins). Not all electric shavers will fit hotel and game-park plug points; visitors should seek advice about adaptors from a local electrical supplier.

Weights and Measures

South Africa uses the metric system.

Power to the People

Eskom, the country's power supply utility, produces over 60 per cent of electricity generated in Africa, exports to neighbours, meets 97 per cent of domestic demand, and plans to connect every South African household to the power grid. Coal is the main source, though Eskom also operates hydroelectric and gas-turbine plants and a nuclear power station. It has also built three huge synfuel plants, which supply 35 per cent of domestic needs and represent the world's first and, as yet, only commercially viable oil-from-coal enterprise. Offshore oil and gas deposits have been located off the south coasts, and the existence of larger fields off Saldanha on the West Coast were confirmed in 2003; currently Mossgas produces 30,000 barrels a day, and 1.5 million tons of natural gas and 250,000 tons of condensate a year. Eskom appears to be on the brink of a land-mark breakthrough in the realms of renewable energy (solar power, at 10 per cent the cost experts considered attainable) and nuclear energy (pebble bed reactors, producing power at four-sevenths of current cost).

Travel Tips

Medical Matters

Visitors to South Africa are responsible for their own arrangements, and are urged to take out medical insurance before departure. Private doctors are listed in the telephone directory under 'Medical Practitioners'. Hospitalization is usually arranged through a medical practitioner, but in an emergency a visitor may telephone or go directly to the casualty department of a General (public) Hospital (listed under 'H' in the local telephone directory). Public hospitals tend to be very crowded and the staff are invariably overworked (although they do manage to maintain surprisingly high standards of treatment and care). Private hospitals generally offer more comfort and individual attention, but are a lot more expensive.

AIDS: The incidence of HIV infection and AIDS-related diseases has increased dramatically over the past number of years and threatens to reach critical proportions. The South African authorities were originally slow to recognize the extent of the crisis, and also slow to act, but they eventually launched a credible publicity and prevention programme. The risk of contracting HIV, though, is no greater in South Africa than in any other country, provided the standard precautions are taken.

Malaria: This disease is prevalent in the Limpopo Province, Mpumalanga, and Northern KwaZulu-Natal. If you're planning to visit one of these areas, embark on a course of anti-malaria tablets before starting out. Tablets are available from local pharmacies, however, some are only available on prescription, so make sure you visit a pharmacist well in advance of your trip. Many prophylactics have to be taken a week before visiting an infested area, and medication continues for up to six weeks after. Note that some strains of this disease are becoming immune to chloroquine (a common anti-malarial drug) so use a substitute prophylactic.

Bilharzia: Also known as schistosomiasis, this debilitating water-borne disease is caused by a parasitical worm common in the lower-lying northern and eastern regions. Be circumspect about swimming in rivers and dams unless the assurances are clear that they are bilharzia free. (Tap water is, however, perfectly safe to drink.)

Creepy crawlies: South Africa has its fair share of snakes, spiders, scorpions and sundry stinging insects, but surprisingly few travellers, even those on safari, suffer serious attack or even discomfort. Those spending a holiday in the bush, or on walking trails, should be more wary, and follow the advice of their ranger or group leader. For protection against ticks (the small red, hard-backed one can transmit tick-bite fever), wear long trousers on walks through long grass and use insect repellant on legs and arms.

Safety and Security

The transition to a democratic order in South Africa has in many ways proved traumatic; there is a great deal of poverty around, and the crime rate in some areas is high. Take the same precautions as you would, say, in central New York; don't walk alone at night in either city or suburb; avoid deserted and poorer areas, unless you're with a group; don't carry large sums of cash around with you; don't leave valuables in your room (use the hotel's safety-deposit box).

Emergencies

The national number for an ambulance and other medical treatment is ☎ 10177 and for a police emergency response unit (Flying Squad) is ☎ 10111, while the emergency number from a mobile or cellphone is ☎ 112. National Enquiries: ☎ 10212.

It is advisable to keep these numbers handy when travelling, but they should only be used if the caller believes life, limb or property is being threatened.

Among the personal crisis help services on offer in South Africa are Lifeline, Childline and Alcoholics Anonymous; all are usually listed in the regional telephone directories.

Language
South Africa has no fewer than 11 official languages, but in most regions (except for the isolated rural areas) English and Afrikaans may at least be understood (Zulu and Xhosa are the most commonly spoken languages). The official languages are:
- English
- Afrikaans
- Zulu
- Xhosa
- Sepedi
- ThsiVenda
- Tsonga
- Siswati
- Sesotho
- Setswana
- Ndebele

INDEX OF SIGHTS

Page numbers given in **bold** type indicate photographs

GENERAL INDEX